ALL ABOUT CATERING

Julia Reay

PITMAN
150
YEARS

PITMAN PUBLISHING
128 Long Acre, London WC2E 9AN

© Julia Reay 1988

First published in Great Britain 1988

British Library Cataloguing in Publication Data
Reay, Julia E.
    All about catering.
    1. Caterers and catering.
    I. Title
    642'.4   TX943

    ISBN 0–273–02830–8

Printed and bound in Great Britain

CONTENTS

PREFACE

This book will give you a very good idea of what is involved in both catering training and a catering career. It contains all the basic information needed to gain an understanding of work in the Hotel and Catering Industry.

All about Catering will be particularly useful for students on school, college or work-related programmes, which are linked to TVEI (Technical, Vocational, Educational Initiative) or CPVE (Certificate Prevocational Education) such as the City and Guilds Catering Foundation Courses, and for City and Guilds 700 Series – Specific Skills courses – and 705, 706_1, 707_1, 706_2 and BTEC FIRST Certificate and Diploma. It will also help those who are wondering whether a Hotel & Catering career will suit them.

The Hotel and Catering Industry has grown enormously over the last few years and today it offers a varied and exciting range of careers in food and accommodation outlets of all kinds. With a basic training in catering it is possible to move around the industry and develop personal interests, and to gain experience on which to build a successful career. The world of catering is a demanding one, calling for students and trainees with stamina, determination and a welcoming personality. Serving the public well is usually a pleasant and satisfying business, but it can also be difficult. Starting out in catering can seem a daunting business. There is so much to learn, and so little time to do it.

Training can be found in many ways, through work experience and company training programmes, college training, or a combination of these. Today there is a course to suit everyone, whether you plan to work in a take-away or a top-class international hotel. Whichever path you choose, this book will help you to quickly gain the basic knowledge and job skills you need to lay a sure foundation for a successful career in this very popular industry.

ACKNOWLEDGMENTS

I wish to acknowledge the help of my colleagues who offered useful ideas and information and gave valuable assistance in checking the manuscript.

Particular thanks to: Robert Henchoz, Iris Jones, Gill Marshall and Tommy Wright.
E Coaney & Co Ltd, Birmingham;
Modern Kitchen Equipment Company of Liverpool for information on catering equipment.

Many thanks to the following who have provided and given permission to reproduce illustrations for this book:

Alexandra Workwear plc
BUPA
Dairy Crest Foods
Falcon Catering Equipment
Foster Refrigerator Ltd
Gilbert Ltd
Hobart Manufacturing Ltd
Jackson Catering Equipment
Kaymet Ltd
Meat and Livestock Commission
Merrychef Ltd
Michael Oliver and Associates
Moorwood Vulcan Ltd
Nilfisk
Robin Wiggins
RoSPA – Royal Society for the Prevention of Accidents
Samuel Groves and Co Ltd
Townsend Thoresen
Trusthouse Forte plc
Vileda Ltd
Wimpy International Ltd
Zanussi CLV Systems Ltd

1 YOU AND THE CATERING INDUSTRY

> Expectations from going into catering – what will I get paid?
> Practical and social skills required in catering
> Catering outlets and employment openings
> The jobs

Expectations from going into catering

Whenever people eat, drink and sleep away from home, they need someone to provide a meal, some refreshment and a bed for the night.

These customers or guests could be on holiday, on a business trip, or on an evening out, at work or school, in hospital or the armed forces, etc.

As these situations arise all round the world a Hotel and Catering training acts as an international passport to interesting work. This is an expanding industry which now includes leisure, sport, travel and tourism.

What can you expect from the Hotel and Catering Industry?

Companionship and friendship
- As part of a team carrying out a large part of their work activity in front of the guests or customers, co-operation and joint activity is both essential and satisfying.
- Fellow workers will respect your effort as you make your contribution to the success of the team.
- Friendship will develop between members of the team who support and rely on each other in the achievement of the team goal and the maintenance of standards.

Conditions
- Reasonable hours of work and holidays – usually 40–45 hours per week spread over a variety of shift patterns, straight shifts, split shifts, alternating early and late shifts.
  This flexible arrangement of working hours gives variety to the pattern of free time for social activity.
- Good working conditions as required by the Health and Safety at Work Act will be the general rule.
- A wide range of small and large establishments gives variety in the working environment. Each sector, e.g. hotel, hospital, school, has its own style and type of organisation.

Job satisfaction
- The opportunity to use your own creative ability and to develop individual ideas.
- Pride in reaching a high standard of performance.
- Varied work.
- A wide range of interesting customers.
- The satisfaction of meeting the challenge of a constantly changing and busy working situation.
- The challenge of trying to improve your skills.
- The opportunity to see a job through from start to finish.
- The chance to take responsibility for both the job and other members of staff.

Pay
- Wages vary greatly across the Hotel & Catering Industry.
- All basic wage rates must be seen in relation to the perks which may be paid as an addition. Basic rates may at first sight seem low but with the addition of free laundry, uniforms, tips, free meals, special accommodation and transport rates, may in fact provide a good overall level of pay.
- The rate of pay and perks will be fixed for each grade of job and will be included in the contract.
- The amount of pay will be based on the hours actually worked or agreed. These will usually be recorded on a 'signing in' sheet or a clock card. The actual amount in the wage packet will be the total wage earned, less deductions for tax and insurance and accommodation if you are 'living in'.
- Check job adverts in local papers, trade magazines, and the job centre for current rates of pay and conditions.
- Future pay prospects will be tied to promotion or the level of job achieved.
  Skilled or supervisory/management staff can expect good rates of pay or salary.

Promotion
- Promotion will be achieved by those who:
  (a) Work steadily and hard, and to a good standard.
  (b) Plan and gain a wide range of experience.
  (c) Undertake suitable on-the-job or college training and qualifications.
- Internal promotion is possible in large companies but it will be necessary to move from one job to another to achieve promotion progress from the smaller work situation. (*See* pages 15–21.)
- A lot is expected from workers in the Hotel and Catering Industry, but if you show that you are capable, promotion will quickly follow. It is not unusual for young workers to be given responsibility for shift teams or the operation of a small unit. Be prepared to take these opportunities and be willing to learn how to cope with a new work requirement.

Training

- The Hotel and Catering Industry offers a variety of ways to undertake continuing training for both personal and skills development. (*See* page 160.)

    The greatest satisfaction will come from the performance of the job itself, the range of customers and the huge variety of establishments in which it is possible to work.

    Giving customer satisfaction will also give you great personal satisfaction.

Practical and social skills required in catering

Practical and social skills go hand in hand in the performance of any kind of Hotel and Catering work activity. They are of equal importance.

Practical skills (technical skills), make it possible for you to do a good job and to produce the right items or service to a high standard.

Social skills affect the way you present yourself to the customers and to the people you work with.

Practical skills

Practical skills used in food preparation, food and beverage service and cleaning and maintenance involve:

Production and service skills
- Performing a particular job using hand skills or machine skills.
- Producing a wide range of food items or performing a set of service, cleaning or maintenance activities.
- Organising your work to gain a good quality result, using the best method and the shortest time.
- Observing a situation and acting correctly to give good customer service.

Selling skills
- Representing the company with pride at all times to help in its success.
- Informing guests of the facilities available.
- Passing on company sales literature.
- Suggesting to customers different items they may wish to buy.
- Telling customers of any special discounts or promotions on offer now or in the future.
- Knowing about activities or places of interest in the area.

    These practical skills will be developed through training and on-the-job experience.

Social skills

Social skills used in the production and service activity cover:

Personal skills
- Looking good at all times to give pleasure to guests and present a good image for the workplace. Wearing correct and well-kept uniform.
- Giving detailed attention to grooming and personal hygiene.

- Welcoming customers with a friendly smile. Remembering the names of guests.
- Giving special attention to the needs of guests with particular requirements: the very young, older customers, and handicapped guests.
- Treating customers and other workers with respect.
- Handling all problems and questions quickly and pleasantly – even complaints.
- Being patient, tactful and diplomatic at all times.
- Making it clear that the customers' satisfaction is also your satisfaction.

Communication skills
- Using a confident and friendly approach.
- Speaking clearly (not overloud).
- Listening with full attention and interest.
- Keeping answers short, accurate and interesting.
- Avoiding boring the customers.
- Recording all information to make sure requests are dealt with.
- Enquiring whether customers are comfortable and are enjoying their room or meal.

Social skills will be developed through observation, training and practice.

Catering outlets and employment openings

Armed Forces

Army, Airforce and Navy   All three services feed and accommodate a large number of personnel in Britain and abroad. Food production covers mass feeding, field cooking, quick food operations, high class and functions catering. Training is offered in all the specialist areas of food production, including baking and butchery. It is possible to gain civilian qualifications, e.g. C & G, 706–1, 706–2, and 706–3. The forces accommodation covers mess, camp, officers' and visitors' accommodation.

Armed Forces

Food production		Food and beverage service		Accommodation	
Call order cook	√	Counter service assistants	√	Domestic assistants	√
Chefs	√	Bar service staff/cellar	√	Housekeeping assistants	√
Cooks	√	Food service staff	√	Room attendants	√
General assistants	√	Vending machine operator	√	Housekeeping supervisors	√
Stores assistants	√	Waiters/waitresses	√		
Catering supervisor	√	Rest/DR supervisors	√		

Commercial

Office/store catering   Large stores provide restaurants for the general public and for their staff. In both cases the demand is usually for a reasonably priced, quickly served satisfying meal, snack or drink. It is common to find a cafeteria style of service in both staff and public restaurants.

In some cases the price of staff meals is subsidised by the company. Stores may also offer specialist restaurant or tea-room facilities.

Large office blocks are generally serviced by a main cafeteria for full meals and snacks and vending machines spread around the building for drinks, biscuits and sweets.

Commercial

Food production		Food and beverage service		Accommodation	
Call order cook	√	Counter service assistants	√	Domestic assistants	√
Chefs	√	Bar service staff/cellar	√	Housekeeping assistants	
Cooks	√	Food service staff	√	Room attendants	
General assistants	√	Vending machine operator	√	Housekeeping supervisors	
Stores assistants	√	Waiters/waitresses	√		
Catering supervisor	√	Rest/DR supervisors	√		

Cafés

Transport, town centre, snack bar or milk bar. Cafés generally offer a quick and inexpensive snack and hot drinks service to people who don't require a full or elaborate meal. They are generally situated on main road routes or town centres where they satisfy the needs of drivers and shoppers. Cafés owned and operated by national companies offer a standard style of décor as well as a standard menu and prices.

Cafés

Food production		Food and beverage service		Accommodation	
Call order cook	√	Counter service assistants	√	Domestic assistants	
Chefs	√	Bar service staff/cellar	√	Housekeeping assistants	
Cooks	√	Food service staff	√	Room attendants	
General assistants	√	Vending machine operator	√	Housekeeping supervisors	
Stores assistants	√	Waiters/waitresses	√		
Catering supervisor	√	Rest/DR supervisors	√		

Conference centres

These will vary in size from a small centre which offers accommodation, meals and a meeting room for as few as 12 people, to a large complex of bedrooms, restaurants, conference rooms, cinema, sports and recreation facilities and display halls. Large companies maintain conference centres for regional meetings and training.

The major conference centres will usually be privately owned and will be hired for a special purpose, e.g. political party conferences.

Conference Centres

Food production		Food and beverage service		Accommodation	
Call order cook		Counter service assistants		Domestic assistants	√
Chefs	√	Bar service staff/cellar	√	Housekeeping assistants	√
Cooks	√	Food service staff	√	Room attendants	√
General assistants	√	Vending machine operator		Housekeeping supervisors	√
Stores assistants	√	Waiters/waitresses	√		
Catering supervisor	√	Rest/DR supervisors	√		

Contract catering

Contract caterers offer a service to any establishment which calls them in to run the catering operation. Schools, industry, hospitals all use the services of contract caterers who take total responsibility for the operation of the catering service and the staff who run it.

The contract catering company will negotiate with the particular school or industrial company a total price which covers all the cost of staff, raw materials, overheads, and profit required to cover the catering service.

The contract company will introduce its own system for organising, recording and controlling the catering operation.

The contract arrangement can be terminated according to previous agreement if either the contractor or the host company are not satisfied. (Contract cleaning companies operate in the same way.)

Contract catering

Food production		Food and beverage service		Accommodation	
Call order cook	√	Counter service assistants	√	Domestic assistants	
Chefs	√	Bar service staff/cellar	√	Housekeeping assistants	
Cooks	√	Food service staff	√	Room attendants	
General assistants	√	Vending machine operator	√	Housekeeping supervisors	
Stores assistants	√	Waiters/waitresses	√		
Catering supervisor	√	Rest/DR supervisors	√		

Fast food/take-away

Fast food is the term used to describe any type of food which is quickly finished to customer demand and which can be 'eaten in the hand'. It covers a wide range of food from burgers, pasties, toasted sandwiches, pizzas, hot dogs, fish and chips.

The well-known fast food companies plan in detail the layout of their fast food counters, the timing and method of assembling and finishing food and the quality and price of the ingredients, and the national advertising. Those who wish to operate a similar kind of fast food outlet can buy this planning in the form of a franchise. Having bought the

Wimpy fast food/take-away

franchise they agree to keep up the standards of the company and to pay a proportion of all profit to the company who sold them the franchise.

A new form of fast food operation is based on the process of freeze/chill. Food items are prepared in bulk and then portioned. They are quickly blast chilled and held in the chiller display cabinet for not more than 4–6 days. The customer chooses an item from the chill display. This is then reheated in a microwave oven for immediate use. The items can be vended and reheated using either counter service or cash-vending with chiller display and microwave oven.

Fast food

Food production		Food and beverage service		Accommodation
Call order cook	√	Counter service assistants	√	Domestic assistants
Chefs	√	Bar service staff/cellar		Housekeeping assistants
Cooks	√	Food service staff	√	Room attendants
General assistants	√	Vending machine operator	√	Housekeeping supervisors
Stores assistants		Waiters/waitresses	√	
Catering supervisor	√	Rest/DR supervisors		

Hospital catering and private clinics

The National Health Service operates its own carefully controlled food production and service system. Attention is given to quality of ingredients, maintenance of nutritional value, appearance and cost.

The range of catering services in a hospital will cover patients' ward dining rooms, trolley service, diets and special needs, or central plate service. Staff – nursing and support staff – restaurants, cafeteria, salad and fast food bars. Also visitors' snack and fast food units, meetings, functions and formal menus.

The hospital service offers on-the-job training and college release schemes for C & G craft qualifications and its own training programmes for supervisors and managers.

Contract catering companies operate in some hospitals at present, covering the same aspects of catering services and with the same aim: to maintain the balance of quality, cost and service. Contracts are being awarded to contract catering companies to run a range of hospital services, e.g. catering, accommodation and laundry services. The company submits a 'competitive tender' which will be accepted if it offers efficiency and economy. The same range of jobs is available to staff who are employed directly by the contract company rather than the National Health Service. Private clinics will generally be smaller than NHS hospitals and will be committed to satisfy the patients' demands in line with the extra payment patients are making for the 'hotel services' aspect of their hospital treatment.

A wider range of food items will be requested and produced but the idea of offering good meals in order to help the patients' progress will be the same as in NHS and contract catering operations.

Hospital staff canteen

Hospitals

Food production		Food and beverage service		Accommodation	
Call order cook	√	Counter service assistants	√	Domestic assistants	√
Chefs	√	Bar service staff/cellar		Housekeeping assistants	√
Cooks	√	Food service staff	√	Room attendants	√
General assistants	√	Vending machine operator		Housekeeping supervisors	√
Stores assistants	√	Waiters/waitresses	√		
Catering supervisor	√	Rest/DR supervisors	√		

Hotels

Hotel operations cover catering, accommodation, reception, bars and maintenance operations. The range of hotels covers the 1500 room city centre computer-controlled operations to the 6–8 bedroom country or seaside hotel. Whatever the size, the services to be covered are the same. However the guest will get more or less personal treatment depending on the amount they pay for the accommodation. Particular hotels may choose to put the emphasis on either the accommodation or the food aspect of the operation.

It is becoming more common for large hotels to operate a 'coffee shop' or quite separate restaurant. Many hotels let out their accommodation for functions, conferences and large product promotions. They also provide club, health, beauty and recreation facilities.

Restaurant area of a Trusthouse Forte hotel

The large hotel groups will operate computer booking, buying, stock and control systems which are identical in each hotel run by that particular company.

The small hotel is more likely to develop its own individual style and form of service, but it too will be aided by business machinery and a limited computer facility in its booking, accounting and control system.

Hotels

Food production		Food and beverage service		Accommodation	
Call order cook		Counter service assistants		Domestic assistants	√
Chefs	√	Bar service staff/cellar	√	Housekeeping assistants	√
Cooks	√	Food service staff	√	Room attendants	√
General assistants	√	Vending machine operator		Housekeeping supervisors	√
Stores assistants	√	Waiters/waitresses	√		
Catering supervisor	√	Rest/DR supervisors	√		

Industry

Industrial catering is undertaken either by the company itself or by a contract caterer employed by the company.

The range of feeding provision will cover a works dining room – either central or spread around – a large site, office and support staff restaurants and directors' and visitors' dining rooms.

The provision in both workers' dining rooms and staff restaurants is likely to cover conventional meals, grills, salads, snacks and fast food and beverages, and will offer either subsidised or cost-controlled meals and quick service.

A wider range of high class foods is likely to be served in the directors' and visitors' dining rooms as a large amount of business will be discussed and arranged over the meal table. The atmosphere created in the dining room will be a positive help to the development of business contacts and therefore plays an important part in the companys' future success.

Industry

Food production		Food and beverage service		Accommodation	
Call order cook	√	Counter service assistants	√	Domestic assistants	
Chefs	√	Bar service staff/cellar		Housekeeping assistants	
Cooks	√	Food service staff	√	Room attendants	
General assistants	√	Vending machine operator	√	Housekeeping supervisors	
Stores assistants	√	Waiters/waitresses	√		
Catering supervisor	√	Rest/DR supervisors	√		

Licensed houses, public houses and wine bars

Licensed houses and public houses usually concentrate on the sale of beer, wines and spirits. They are subject to licensing laws which control their opening hours. Increasingly both are providing bar snacks and limited meal service to accompany the sale of drinks. They may offer a cold buffet and speciality of the house or a chill/microwave or freeze/microwave hot snack service.

Wine bars set out to balance the sale of food and wine and to prepare items of food which will enhance the enjoyment of the wine.

All three food and drink outlets also offer an off-licence or take-away drink sales facility.

Licensed houses

Food production		Food and beverage service		Accommodation	
Call order cook	√	Counter service assistants	√	Domestic assistants	√
Chefs		Bar service staff/cellar		Housekeeping assistants	√
Cooks		Food service staff		Room attendants	
General assistants		Vending machine operator		Housekeeping supervisors	
Stores assistants		Waiters/waitresses	√		
Catering supervisor		Rest/DR supervisors			

Outside catering

This includes outdoor, shows, sports events and private house functions.

Outside catering service operations take the prepared or part-prepared food, equipment and staff to the place where an event or function is being held. This could be a marquee, a caravan or a van kitchen, a community hall, town hall or a private house.

Outside caterers usually employ a small group of permanent staff to carry out basic preparation, crating, transporting, and costing of function items. These staff are supplemented by casual PT staff who are employed to meet the demand of the function, depending on the size and scope. The casual staff are generally drawn from those on the regular *on-call* list held by the outside caterer.

Outside catering

Food production		Food and beverage service		Accommodation	
Call order cook		Counter service assistants		Domestic assistants	
Chefs	√	Bar service staff/cellar		Housekeeping assistants	
Cooks	√	Food service staff	√	Room attendants	
General assistants	√	Vending machine operator		Housekeeping supervisors	
Stores assistants		Waiters/waitresses	√		
Catering supervisor	√	Rest/DR supervisors	√		

Recreation, leisure, sports centres, health farms and social clubs

These establishments usually offer non-residents facilities and concentrate on the recreation or leisure aspects which are serviced by a range of food outlets and some accommodation services, e.g. laundry and cleaning of special areas. The feeding provision will cover bars; salad and snack, and hot drinks and full restaurant facilities. Health farms will offer residential accommodation.

In areas where food is considered to be part of the treatment, as in the health farm, special attention will be given to nutritional content, style of preparation and timing of the service.

Social clubs may hire out their facilities to functions either on a full catering or client self-catering basis.

Where the clubs are offering a catering service they will have a range of standard priced menus from which the client can choose the most suitable meal for their needs, at a given price.

Recreation/leisure

Food production		Food and beverage service		Accommodation	
Call order cook	√	Counter service assistants	√	Domestic assistants	√
Chefs	√	Bar service staff/cellar	√	Housekeeping assistants	√
Cooks	√	Food service staff	√	Room attendants	√
General assistants	√	Vending machine operator		Housekeeping supervisors	√
Stores assistants	√	Waiters/waitresses	√		
Catering supervisor	√	Rest/DR supervisors	√		

Restaurants

Restaurants exist only for the production and service of food. They vary not only in size but also in style and price range.

A restaurant will choose a theme, menu style and price band to suit the type of customer they wish to attract and at the same time to show off the particular expertise of their cooks and chefs. Where a restaurant specialises in a particular type of food, e.g. Italian or vegetarian, it is known as a speciality restaurant.

Restaurants may operate on a fixed choice menu (table d'hôte) or a free choice menu (à la Carte). The fixed choice menu will usually be priced for the complete meal. A free choice menu will have each individual item priced. A meal of the day, 'chef's special', or 'plat du jour', may be attached to either a table d'hôte or à la carte menu. It is necessary for all restaurants to display the price of items clearly to the customers before they place their order.

In restaurant operations the production of food, service of food and service of wine share equal importance in the creation of a good meal experience and customer satisfaction.

Restaurants

Food production		Food and beverage service		Accommodation	
Call order cook		Counter service assistants		Domestic assistants	
Chefs	√	Bar service staff/cellar	√	Housekeeping assistants	
Cooks	√	Food service staff	√	Room attendants	
General assistants	√	Vending machine operator		Housekeeping supervisors	
Stores assistants	√	Waiters/waitresses	√		
Catering supervisor	√	Rest/DR supervisors	√		

Schools, colleges and universities

Schools, colleges, and universities with residential pupils and students will operate both food and accommodation services. Meals will usually be served at set times using cafeteria 'help yourself' or table service. Where cafeteria service is used a varied choice of main and snack items will be offered.

Some colleges and universities provide self-catering facilities: as well as casual feeding provision. Here the students can choose whether to buy a meal in the central restaurant or snack area or prepare his or her own food.

In day-schools and colleges meal, snack and beverage services are usually provided either at set periods as in school or all day as in colleges, using cafeteria and vending service systems. An economic price is charged for all food items.

Private schools and colleges will either control their own catering services or employ a contract catering company. State schools and colleges catering services are usually run or monitored by the local Education Authority schools and college catering service.

Schools, colleges and universities

Food production		Food and beverage service		Accommodation	
Call order cook		Counter service assistants		Domestic assistants	√
Chefs	√	Bar service staff/cellar		Housekeeping assistants	√
Cooks	√	Food service staff	√	Room attendants	√
General assistants	√	Vending machine operator		Housekeeping supervisors	√
Stores assistants	√	Waiters/waitresses	√		
Catering supervisor	√	Rest/DR supervisors	√		

Transport catering

Air Food for flights is prepared in factory conditions in production units on the ground. It is carefully controlled for variety, quality and hygiene to match the problems of transporting the food and holding it at the correct temperature until needed. Reheating and service are in-flight to meet the customers' needs, whatever time of day or night the meal is eaten and whatever the nationality of the diner.

Rail Rail catering has two main aspects: *station provision* – buffet, snack bar, restaurant and drinks shop; and *train provision*; meal service, buffet bar and drinks service.

Station restaurants, bar and snack outlets run like any other commercial food concern and need to attract not only travelling customers, but those meeting the travellers or coming in from offices and shops around the station area. They may have to provide some of the services for a full 24 hour day.

The provision of food for service on trains involves a complex process of pre-ordering items, packing the train with snacks and pre-prepared goods and then finishing hot items while the train journey is in progress. The kitchen space on the train in very limited, and is designed with great care to make maximum use of the space and to provide an area which is both safe and easy to work in.

Sea Ferries, liners and cargo boats of all sizes carry a great many passengers on both short and long journeys. As it is impossible to obtain food other than from the ship itself it is important that all of the passenger and

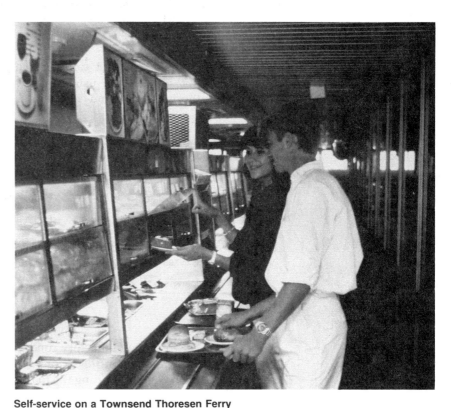

Self-service on a Townsend Thoresen Ferry

crew needs are taken care of. Restaurant snack and drinks facilities will be in demand. On pleasure cruises or long journeys food becomes part of the entertainment for passengers and becomes a feature of the journey. In these circumstances and where passenger charges are high the meals will be elaborate. Provisioning a ship and controlling the issue of supplies is a major job, particularly where local supplies are taken on at foreign ports.

Full accommodation services are also needed on large and small ships for both crew and passengers.

Transport catering

Food production		Food and beverage service		Accommodation	
Call order cook	√	Counter service assistants	√	Domestic assistants	√
Chefs	√	Bar service staff/cellar	√	Housekeeping assistants	
Cooks	√	Food service staff	√	Room attendants	√
General assistants	√	Vending machine operator	√	Housekeeping supervisors	
Stores assistants	√	Waiters/waitresses	√		
Catering supervisor	√	Rest/DR supervisors	√		

The jobs

Call order cooks

On-the-job training:	√
Qualifications needed:	C & G 700/1

The call order cook's job covers all aspects of assembly, finishing, and presentation of food to meet the immediate orders of the customer. Pre-prepared food items are made ready for service using microwave or convection oven, grill, fryer or griddle. The work also involves the preparation and presentation of cold food.

Emphasis is put on hygienic handling of food and customer satisfaction achieved through the careful, tactful and good-humoured manner of the call order cook.

Attention to health and safety detail is also important.

Chefs/cooks

On-the-job training:	√ and HCTB
Qualifications needed:	C & G 705
	C & G 706_1
	C & G 706_2
	C & G 706_3
	C & G 771
	BTEC FIRST and NATIONAL CERT/DIP

Chef's, or cooks' duties will vary according to the level of experience they have and the type of establishment in which they work.

Duties will cover the preparation of food in the meat, fish, vegetables, sweet/pastry and preparation sections of the production unit.

A chef or cook may choose to specialise and become more skilled in a single area of the work, e.g. sweets/pastry preparation.

Modern chefs or cooks will be required to use new techniques of food preparation, e.g. preparation of batch food for freezing/chilling as well as the more traditional methods.

They will work in conjunction with the catering manager to plan menus, decide on preparation, portions, and presentation procedures, order raw ingredients and calculate the selling price of items.

Chefs or cooks work as part of a team and they will co-ordinate the activity of the assistant chefs/cooks who also work as part of the team.

The maintenance of hygienic practices and procedures, the upkeep of safe working conditions and the maintenance of high standards of food production are all important parts of their activity.

General assistant/kitchen porter

On-the-job training:	√
Qualifications needed:	None

General assistants in the food production area will assist with all cleaning and maintenance procedures which relate to the care of both large and small equipment.

They will be required to understand and apply safety and hygiene regulations and to follow the work pattern and procedures laid down by the supervisor.

General assistants may be expected to carry out some general food preparation activity.

Porters will be required to move heavy items under the direction of the head chef or catering supervisor and undertake cleaning and up-keep of the main working area, kitchen store, office and cloakroom and waste disposal areas.

Stores assistant

On-the-job training: √

Qualifications needed: None

The stores assistant will be required to assist in the receipt and stacking of stores goods and to keep to stock rotation patterns and record all items issued. It will be necessary to take great care with the weighing of food items and the maintenance of hygienic conditions within the storage area. Attention to the security of the goods to prevent loss or pilferage is most important.

The assistant will be expected to work under the direction of the storekeeper at all times.

Catering supervisor

On-the-job training: √ and HCTB

Qualifications needed: C & G 706_2 & NEBSS or C & G   771
BTEC NATIONAL CERT/DIP
BTEC HIGHER CERT/DIP

The catering supervisor is responsible for the planning and co-ordinating of all budgeting, purchasing, storing, production, and service activity within the food production area.

The planning of duty rotas, work and cleaning schedules and training programmes, form a part of the catering supervisor's activity.

Counter service assistant

On-the-job training: √

Qualifications needed: C & G 700_4

The counter service assistant will be required to present and serve food to the cafeteria customer, to keep the food service area in a clean and hygienic condition, to work safely and to re-stock food service points as required.

Portion control and careful measurement are important aspects of the work.

Personal appearance and manner must be good in order to attract customers and add to their enjoyment of the meal experience.

Bar service/cellar operative

On-the-job training:	√

Qualifications needed:	C & G	700_5
	C & G	700_8
	C & G	707_1
	C & G	717

Bar/cellar staff are required to serve drinks, control cash and maintain the bar area in a clean, safe condition. They will require a detailed knowledge of the drinks being served and the ability to change optics, change CO_2 cylinders, change and test cask, keg and tank beers and to handle and change bulk minerals.

General cleaning and maintenance of the public bar area are also the responsibility of the bar/cellar staff.

Personal presentation and manner are of great importance in this area.

Bar staff in a Trusthouse Forte hotel

Food service operative

On-the-job training:	√

Qualifications needed:	C & G	700_3
	C & G	705
	C & G	707_1
	C & G	707_2
	C & G	717

The food service operative will be required to portion and present food to the customer using the particular form of service required, e.g. central plate service or buffet service.

Work will be planned and supervised by the dining room or restaurant supervisor.

The food service operative will be required to take great care with personal appearance, cleanliness and manner when dealing with customers.

Vending machine operator

On-the-job training:	$\vee$
Qualifications needed:	C & G 700_9

Vending machine operators will be required to load and clean the vending machines according to the established programme for filling, care and maintenance.

They will ensure that food commodities are in good condition both in store and when loaded into the machine and that the level of heat and chill in the machine is kept at the correct temperature. The control of coin mechanism and collection of cash may form part of the operator's activity.

Dealing quickly with problems as they occur is a vital part of the job.

Waiter/waitress

On-the-job training:	$\vee$ and HCTB
Qualifications needed:	C & G 705
	C & G 707_1
	C & G 707_2
	C & G 717
	BTEC FIRST CERT/DIP

The waiter or waitress has responsibility for the preparation of the tools and equipment needed during the service period. The crockery, cutlery and tools required will vary according to the type of service which can range from silver service to plate or family service.

It is necessary for the waiter/waitress to know and be able to describe to customers all the items on the menu and wine list.

The waiter takes the customer's order, relays it to the kitchen, collects the order and takes it to a side-table from where the customer is served. The waiter or waitress must use their skill to present the food in an appetising and correctly served manner. The cleaning and maintenance of the working area is also their responsibility.

Restaurant/dining room supervisor

On-the-job training:	$\sqrt{}$ and HCTB

Qualifications needed:	C & G 705
	C & G 707_1
	C & G 707_2
	C & G 717 & NEBSS or C & G 771
	BTEC NATIONAL CERT/DIP
	BTEC HIGHER CERT/DIP

The restaurant or dining room supervisor is responsible for the planning and co-ordination of all staff and work activity within the food service area.

Liaison with the food production unit, control of costs and maintenance of standards are all part of the dining room supervisor's responsibility. Satisfying the needs of the customer is of prime importance.

Domestic assistant

On-the-job training:	$\sqrt{}$

Qualifications needed:	C & G 700_2

A domestic assistant will work as part of a team, undertaking general cleaning duties in both public and specialist areas.

Work will be under the direction and control of a supervisor who will be responsible for day-to-day training and supervision of the domestic assistant.

Attention to safe working procedures and maintenance of high standards of finish are most important in this work.

Housekeeping assistant

On-the-job training:	$\sqrt{}$

Qualifications needed:	C & G 705
	C & G 708
	BTEC FIRST CERT/DIP

The housekeeping assistant will assist the housekeeper by taking responsibilities for the cleaning and upkeep of a particular area of work, e.g. corridor of bedrooms, or a particular aspect of the cleaning and maintenance operation, e.g. use of large or specialised equipment, or the arrangement of rooms for a particular type of booking and use. Work will be carried out under the direction of the housekeeper using the cleaning schedules; work cards and training given. The housekeeping assistant will take care of the cleaning equipment and materials needed and will be aware of the safe forms of operation in order to safeguard fellow workers and guests.

The maintenance of a high standard of finish in all cleaning and preparation activity is most important for the guests' well-being and satisfaction.

Room attendant/room maid

On-the-job training:	$\sqrt{}$
Qualifications needed:	C & G 700_2

The room attendant will assist in the maintenance of public rooms, cloakrooms, corridors, and bedrooms. This will involve general cleaning duties, using both hand and machine methods, replacement of linen and disposal of waste. It also covers deep cleaning and periodic special cleaning activity.

Housekeeping supervisor

On-the-job training:	$\sqrt{}$ and HCTB
Qualifications needed:	C & G 705
	C & G 708 & NEBSS
	BTEC NATIONAL CERT/DIP
	BTEC HIGHER CERT/DIP

The housekeeping supervisor is responsible for the planning and control of all work and staff activity. Control of cleaning materials and equipment and the planning of work duty and training schedules are part of the overall responsibility, along with cost control and the maintenance of high standards.

Training and operation for health and safety, and fire training and procedures, are a vital part of the safety operation of this section.

Hotel reception

On-the-job training:	$\sqrt{}$
Qualifications needed:	Training and experience can be gained through City and Guilds 709 programme or as part of a BTEC NATIONAL CERT/DIP. A good secretarial or general reception qualification will also give entry to this area of work.

The hotel receptionist works as part of a team, alongside food production and service staff, bar, accommodation and portering staff.

The receptionist works at the heart of hotel and catering activity and must have a knowledge of the overall operation of all sections.

The duties of a hotel receptionist cover:
- welcoming customers
- 'selling' facilities and special functions and giving information on local events and places of interest
- recording advance reservations, taken by telephone or letter
- dealing with arrivals and preparing arrival and departure lists either manually or using the computer
- coping with chance guests

- providing information on room occupancy to management, accommodation staff and porters
- recording requests for room service, newspapers, etc.
- dealing with departing guests and paying bills – balancing the day's business
- cashing up from bars and restaurants
- dealing with the switchboard

Personal requirements include:
- common sense
- communication skills
- efficiency and a good memory
- good grooming and appearance
- personality, patience and understanding
- sense of humour
- social skills (see pp 3–4)
- stamina

Note: On-the-job training may be linked to:
1   Company schemes;
2   HCTB programmes;
3   Nationally promoted schemes such as YTS and school link programmes.

2 WORKING IN CATERING

Employment practice
Clothing: work wear
Hygiene
Health and safety
Working in a team: coping with problems

Employment practice

For every employed person there are legal requirements and codes of practice which cover the way both the employer and employee must behave. These legal requirements and agreed practices are usually written into the contract of employment. If either the employer or employee acts against these agreed terms the employment arrangement is in danger of being broken.

The contract must be carefully read and understood by the new worker before signing.

If the job description or conditions of employment change during the working period the contract should be brought up to date to match those changes.

The points described on pp 24–28 are for full-time workers and those on short-term fixed contracts.

There is a separate legal provision for part-time and casual staff. (See pp 28–29.)

Employment acts

Acts which relate to all aspects of employment:
- Employment Protection Act, 1975
- Employment Protection Consolidation Act, 1978
- Trades Union & Labour Relations Act, 1976
- Employment Act, 1982

Acts which relate to special aspects of employment:
- Sex Discrimination Act, 1975
- Race Relations Act, 1976
- Contracts of Employment Act, 1972
- Equal Pay Act, 1970
- Health and Safety at Work Act, 1974

Aspects of employment covered by the above acts:
- disciplinary procedures;
- discrimination on the grounds of race, sex and religion;
- employment contracts;
- equal pay for men and women;
- health and safety;
- maternity rights;
- notice;
- redundancy;
- time off for training, public duties and trades union activities;
- unfair dismissal.

Full-time workers' contracts

Verbal   A spoken (verbal) offer of a job can act as a contract. The contract is confirmed, by the action of the employee starting work. Problems may arise about the actual meaning of the words spoken and the correct detail agreed. It is usual to confirm in writing at a later date the conditions of service which have been agreed verbally.

Written   A written contract is a full and binding agreement between the employer and the new worker. It is read, agreed and signed by both of them. Any changes made to the contract must be agreed between the employer and the worker and *not* dictated by one of them alone.

All workers who are employed for 16 hours or more a week must be given a written statement setting out all their employment details, not more than 13 weeks after starting work. A written statement need not be a full contract of employment, but it must include all the important terms of service.

Written notice must be given to the worker, one month in advance, before any changes are made to the contents of the written statement.

Items to be included in a contract

Duties – the job itself   To include:
1   The name of the job: job title.
2   The place where the job is to be done.
3   All job activities which the worker is expected to cover, e.g. food production, food service, cleaning and maintenance.
4   Any other duties which are not directly part of the job but which the worker can be called on to do in case of staff absence or emergency.

Wage   To include:
1   The salary scale or wage rate for the job.
2   The job grade or scale.
3   Method of paying, e.g. cash or cheque.
4   Frequency of payment: weekly/monthly.
5   Wage statement.

Money matters   *Deductions* – To include:
1 National insurance.
2 Tax.
3 Pension.
4 Board and lodging.
5 Meals on duty.
6 Maintenance of uniform.

Holiday pay – To include:
1 The rate to be paid for agreed holiday allowance.
2 Arrangements for holiday without pay.

Overtime – To include:
1 The amount of overtime which can be expected.
2 The arrangements for overtime hours.
3 Details of overtime rates of pay.
4 Arrangements for taking compensation time off in lieu of overtime pay.

Pension – To include:
1 The company pension scheme provision and rate of contribution.
2 Details of those who can take part in the scheme.

Sickness pay – To include:
1 The company policy on days off with pay allowed for sickness.
2 The procedure for claiming sick pay.

Security of goods and premises   *Company search rights* – To include:
1 A declaration that the company are free to search workers.
2 Details of who is authorised to carry out the search.
3 The time, place and conditions where the search will be carried out.

Personal property – To include:
A statement warning workers that the company has no responsibility for personal property unless it is kept in the locked locker provided, or in the case of valuables, handed to the supervisor or manager to be stored in a safe.

Presence on premises – To include:
1 The times when a worker is expected to be on the premises as part of their work.
2 The times when a worker is not allowed on the premises or a particular part of the premises, e.g. the public rooms, lounges and bars.

Settling work problems   *Disciplinary procedures*
The procedure which must be followed when disciplinary rules have been broken: the rules as laid down in the contract.
A disciplinary procedure usually follows the sequence of:

- a first verbal warning for a minor offence;
- a first written warning which includes a set time allowed for the worker to improve his behaviour;
- notice is finally given.

At any time the employer can break off the disciplinary process if the worker is seen to make a genuine effort to improve either performance or behaviour.

Disciplinary rules
The general offences for which the disciplinary procedure will be used, e.g. poor time-keeping, poor work, bad behaviour, ignoring safety procedures, stealing, behaving unhygienically, smoking on duty, failing to dress properly.

Grievance procedures   –   To include:
1   The type of problem a worker may consider to be a grievance (e.g. a major work problem that needs sorting out; work disagreement with colleagues; inadequate equipment etc.)
2   The procedure for bringing the grievance to the attention of the management.
A grievance procedure usually follows a pattern. The worker will:
- First take the problem to the supervisor or head of department who will try to solve it. The worker is free to take a friend.
- If the grievance is still not solved it is passed forward to the head of department or section leader who will offer solutions after discussion with the worker.
- If the problem is not solved within a set time (e.g. five days) it will be passed to the manager.
- The union representative may be called in to the discussion if this is thought to be of help.

Termination: ending the employment

Dismissal   –   To include:
1   The reasons why dismissal may occur. This will include the worker's conduct, or misconduct, ability to perform the job, health, honesty.
2   The need to dismiss staff through redundancy and the procedure for carrying out the redundancy.
3   The procedure to be used before dismissal occurs, e.g. use of disciplinary procedure.

Unfair dismissal   –   To include:
1   Those who are able to claim unfair dismissal, e.g. workers with one year of continuous service.
2   Acceptable grounds for an unfair dismissal claim, e.g. when contract terms have been broken, or employer has not used correct timing or procedures for carrying out the dismissal.

Notice   –   To include:
1   The arrangements for giving notice when the worker wishes to leave the job.

2   The procedure for the employer to follow when he wishes a worker to leave. The minimum notice an employer must give a worker who has been employed for more than four weeks is:

- one week's notice where the worker has been employed for less than two years.
- one week for each year of service for the worker who has worked full-time for more than two years but less than twelve years.
- twelve weeks for a worker who has worked more than twelve years.
- the worker who has worked for more than four weeks full-time and wishes to leave, has to give one week's notice only.

Working hours and conditions

Hours/time-off – To include:
1   The normal working hours for the worker.
2   The shift arrangements which operate, e.g. straight shift, split shift, alternating shift.
3   Any other variation of the working pattern which can reasonably be required to cover staff absence or emergency.

Holiday allowance – To include:
1   The number of holiday days allowed for each week, year, or month of work.
2   The period of the year during which the holiday must be taken when a choice is offered.
3   The set period when holidays must be taken if the working area shuts down for a fixed time each year.

Maternity leave, ante-natal care
To include the rights of each woman who has worked full-time for the employer for two years. In general it will allow for time off with pay and the right to return to a similar job following the birth of the baby. When leave is to be taken paid time off will be given to workers, for ante-natal care, on presentation of proof that appointments have been made.

Sickness notification
Details of the company's requirements, e.g. self-certification arrangements or need for doctor's certificate for short periods of absence, or 'Fit for Work' certificate following longer periods of absence. (Arrangements vary in different places of work.) The usual arrangement for self-certification is for the worker to collect a self-certification form from the doctor's surgery after three days of continuous illness. The worker completes this form to cover the first week of absence. Following weeks of sickness must be covered by a doctor's note.

The future

Training, promotion and transfer – To include:
1   Brief detail of the company's training policy.
2   An indication of how the worker can apply for training.
3   The promotion policy of the company.
4   Procedure for requesting transfer.

Tax (full time employment)   Your employer will notify the tax office that you have started work. He will ask you to complete a simple coding claim form.

Tax Code
The tax office will issue you with a PAYE code which shows the amount of tax-free pay you are entitled to.

It is important to check your code against the notes supplied with it to ensure that you are not paying too much or too little tax. If at any point you have paid too much tax, it will be refunded to you at the end of the tax year.

A temporary code may be given at the start of employment. This will be adjusted by the tax office as soon as they have details of your earnings.

PAYE (Pay As You Earn)
P45: When you change your job you must collect your P45 (your personal tax record for the year) from your present employer and give it to your new employer. The P45 is your tax leaving certificate.

Tax Holiday Work
(See p. 29 – Pay for part time/temporary or casual staff.)

Part-time, temporary, or casual workers

A part-time or fixed-term contract or written terms of employment may be presented by the employer, stating the detail of the employment relationship between the part-time worker and the employer.

An employer is free to include some of the benefits offered to full-time workers, but this is not at present a legal requirement.

It is likely that, through the influence of the EEC, part-time workers will soon be employed under similar conditions of service as full-time workers.

The Hotel and Catering Industry employs many part-time and seasonal staff to cope economically with seasonal and other variations in demand.

All part-time, temporary or casual workers should know about the following:

Sixteen-hour rule
Anyone who works less than 16 hours a week is regarded as a part-time worker and is *not* entitled to full employment protection. The exception is anyone who has worked for at least eight hours a week for five years.

Conditions
The employer has *no* legal obligation to offer part-time, temporary or casual workers any of the following benefits.
- holiday pay;
- job security;
- maternity pay;
- notice;
- pension;

- protection against unfair dismissal;
- redundancy pay;
- sick pay.

New workers must enquire about each of these points at the time of engagement.

Pay

1   Part-time, temporary or casual workers will be paid, usually, on an hourly rate for work performed.
2   Part-time rates will generally be lower than full-time rates.
3   In most areas of Hotel & Catering operations a minimum wage or hourly rate will be fixed by the wages council.
4   Employers are free to offer a higher rate plus 'perks', e.g. meals on duty and uniforms, if they choose to.
5   Tax will be deducted by the employer.
6   You can claim a refund if your income is too small for tax or you can claim exemption if you are a student.

Promotion

Promotion opportunities are limited for part-time workers. However, workers who move carefully from one part-time job to another, building up sound experience, can prepare themselves for promotion.

Training

Few part-time workers will be given continuous training. All workers can expect to be given Fire, Health, Safety and Hygiene training as well as limited job training.

Job sharing

Job sharing offers the advantages of part-time work:
- extra free time
- flexible working hours

while offering some of the training and promotion possibilities which full-time workers have.

It is still a form of part-time work if each worker is employed for less than 16 hours per week.

However, if each worker is employed for more than 16 hours a week, they will receive full-time benefits on a pro-rata basis to match the number of hours they work.

A job may be shared with another worker on:
1   a shared day basis;
2   a shared week basis (3 days each);
3   a one-week-on/one-week-off basis.

Trades union organisation and the catering worker

The unions which operate in the Industry are:
1   ASTMS   Association of Scientific, Technical and Management Staffs
2   GMWU   General and Municipal Workers Union (incorporates the HCWU – Hotel and Catering Workers Union)

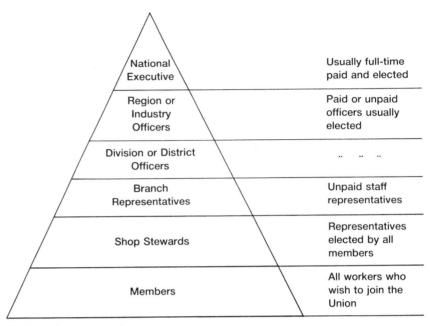

Trades union organisation

3   NALHM   National Association of Licensed House Managers
4   NUPE   National Association of Public Employees
5   TGWU   Transport and General Workers Union
6   TSSA   Transport Salaried Staffs Association
7   USDA   Union of Shop, Distributive and Allied Workers.

Membership of a trades union is open to all catering workers. However, a worker cannot be compelled to join a trades union.

The union will negotiate wages and conditions of work on behalf of the worker and make sure that minimum wage rates are being paid, that working conditions are safe and that contract agreements are kept.

An elected trades union representative negotiates on behalf of members with the management in order to ensure that agreed legal and company regulations are carried out. Representatives are elected by all of the workers who hold union membership. It is usually a worker who is trusted and respected by a large section of the workforce, and who has the ability to think clearly and to use a calm and sensible approach to discussion of important issues.

Clothing: work wear

Work wear is worn for the following reasons:
1   It protects the product or the work activity from contamination by the worker.
2   It protects the worker from contamination by a product, e.g. food or cleaning agent, or work activity, e.g. removing food waste.
3   It acts as a barrier in the prevention of cross-contamination. Different uniforms are provided and used for different purposes.

4   It provides a comfortable and convenient form of uniform with adequate room for movement. It will be made from a suitable material to be strong, light, hygienic and hardwearing while at the same time giving a good appearance.

5   It allows for regular change and replacement to keep good standards of hygiene.

6   It gives a look of tidiness and uniformity to a group of workers. It also gives a clear feeling of the company image and the standards it sets, and acts as 'positive selling' for the company.

Any item of uniform clothing should be worn *only* for the particular job it is allocated for. It should be worn *only* in the working area. When not in use work clothing should be hung up away from outdoor clothing which might contaminate it.

In order to achieve its protective purpose all work wear must be regularly washed, pressed and repaired.

Where the company hires the uniforms the hire company will be responsible for providing regular supplies of clean, repaired uniforms. They will replace items which are worn out or damaged.

Where the company owns the work wear and issues it to workers, they will arrange for washing and repairs to be done unless they give the worker an allowance to cover the cost of maintaining their own uniform.

Where the workers provide their own uniform it is up to them to wash items at home or in the laundry provided at work.

For all types of uniform the best material to choose will be easy care cotton mix. This provides the necessary ventilation for the body's comfort and freshness and the crispness to give a good appearance, however many times the items are washed.

Choice of underwear is as important as the choice of outerwear at work. For hygiene and comfort in the active, hot working situation loose cotton underwear is most suitable as it allows the body to 'breathe' and stay fresh. It absorbs excess perspiration without giving off unpleasant odours.

Work shoes may be provided by employers to make sure that safe footwear is worn. If the individual worker provides shoes they must be made of good quality material, support the foot well, give protection to the top of the foot and have safe soles.

Items of garments

Chef's/cook's hat (male)
- protects hair from effects of heat and steam
- protects food from loose hairs and scurf
- indicates the status of the chef/cook

Fabric	*Care and maintenance*
(*a*) starched cotton	wash, starch and press
(*b*) permanently pleated nylon net	wash regularly, and drip dry
(*c*) disposable paper	dispose of after 7–10 days

Chef's/cook's net or flat hat (female)

- purpose: as above

Fabric
(a) starched white cotton
(b) terylene net
(c) disposable paper

Care and maintenance
as above

Neckerchief

- absorbs excess perspiration

Fabric
(a) white cotton material

Care and maintenance
hot wash and press

Chef's/cook's jacket (male or female)

- protects body from effects of heat, steam and contamination
- long sleeves protect from hot splashes of liquid or fat, and from oven burns
- white garments show up stains and indicate easily when clothes need to be changed

Fabric
(a) white cotton

(b) drip dry
white cotton/terylene mix material

Care and maintenance
soak, hot wash and press while still damp
frequent warm wash, cool rinse, drip dry, no iron.

Chef's/cook's trousers (male/female)

- protects legs from spillage and burns

Fabric
(a) blue and white check cotton

Care and maintenance
soak hot wash, press when still damp

Chef/cook

Waiter

Stores/porter/maintenance! all-in-one trousers (see p. 36)

	(b) white cotton/terylene mix material	frequent warm wash, cool rinse, drip dry, no iron

Chef's/cook's apron (male/female)

- protects against spillage
- a simple item which can be changed regularly and easily to provide good hygiene conditions
- usually full bib type

Fabric	*Care and maintenance*
(a) heavy white cotton	soak, hot wash, starch, press while damp
(b) heavy blue & white stripe cotton material	as above
(c) heavy white cotton/terylene mix material.	frequent warm wash, cool rinse, drip dry, no iron

Chef's/cook's coverall (female)

- protects body from the effects of heat, steam and contamination
- white clothes reflect the heat and cool the body

Fabric	*Care and maintenance*
white cotton/terylene mix material	frequent warm wash, cool rinse, drip dry, no iron

Shoes

- provide comfort and protection for the feet
- firm soles avoid the danger of slipping and tripping

	Care and maintenance
	regular polishing and repair: split soles or damaged heels can cause danger

Waiter's jacket

- gives a crisp and businesslike appearance.
- shows the theme, colour scheme and style of the restaurant or dining-room area
- indicates the type of food service operation being used
- shows the status of the waiter
- any colour to suit the place of work

Fabric	*Care and maintenance*
(a) wool worsted	regular dry clean
(b) terylene/cotton	frequent warm wash, cool rinse, drip dry, no iron

Waiter's trousers

- purpose: as for jacket

Fabric	*Care and maintenance*
as above	as above

Waiter's shirt ● purpose: as for jacket

Fabric *Care and maintenance*
(a) pure cotton hot wash, iron while still damp
(b) cotton mix frequent warm wash, cool rinse,
  drip dry, no iron

Waitress's dress ● purpose: as for jacket
● any colour to suit the requirement of the restaurant or dining room colour plan
● a lace or fabric collar may be added to enhance the appearance

Fabric *Care and maintenance*
cotton/terylene mix frequent warm wash, cool rinse,
  drip dry, no iron

Waitress's skirt   ● purpose: as for jacket

Fabric	Care and maintenance
(a) wool worsted	dry clean
(b) wool/terylene	frequent warm wash, cool rinse,
(c) cotton/terylene	drip dry

Waitress's blouse   ● purpose: as for jacket

Fabric	Care and maintenance
(a) cotton	hot wash, iron damp
(b) cotton/synthetic mix	warm wash, cool rinse, drip dry,
(c) synthetic fabric	no iron

Waitress's apron   ● purpose is mainly decorative to add a fresh and attractive feature to the uniform
      ● protects the food from contamination by the food service worker

Fabric	Care and maintenance
(a) fine cotton and lace or broderie anglaise	warm wash, light starch, iron carefully while still damp
(b) fine terylene and lace	warm wash, cool rinse, drip dry

Food service assistant's jacket (male)   ● protects the food from contamination by the food service worker

Fabric	Care and maintenance
(a) white cotton	hot wash, starch, iron while damp
(b) white cotton terylene mix	warm wash, cool rinse, drip dry

Food service assistant's trousers (male)   ● as for jacket

Food service assistant's coverall (female)   ● protects food from contamination
      ● usually white

Fabric	Care and maintenance
(a) cotton/terylene mix material	Frequent warm wash, cool rinse, drip dry, no iron

Bar service assistant's jacket (male)   ● gives a crisp and businesslike appearance
      ● indicates the worker's position and role
      ● colour to suit the bar theme

Fabric	Care and maintenance
(a) worsted/terylene	frequent warm wash, cool rinse,
(b) cotton/terylene mix	drip dry, no iron

Bar service assistant's dress (female)   ● purpose as above
      ● colour to suit the bar theme

Fabric
any hard wearing material of good
appearance

General assistant's
workcoat (male)
- protects the worker from dirt and contamination
- protects the food or clean area from contamination by the worker
- colour usually white/grey/khaki

Fabric	*Care and maintenance*
(a) cotton/terylene mix	frequent warm wash, cool rinse, drip dry

General assistant's
coverall (female)
- purpose as above
- colour – usually white or pastel check or stripe

Fabric	*Care and maintenance*
(a) cotton/terylene mix	as above

General assistant's
heavy duty apron
(male/female)
- takes heavy soiling and washing
- provides added protection for dirty or dangerous jobs

Fabric	*Care and maintenance*
heavy twill cotton	boil wash, iron when damp, commercial laundry

General assistant's
waterproof apron
(male/female)
- protects from wet soiling and cleaning dirt

Fabric	*Care and maintenance*
(a) cotton/pvc mix (heavy)	wash by damp wiping, dry with
(b) polythene (light)	soft fabric or soft tissue

Stores/porter/
maintenance: all-in-one
trousers/overall
(male/female)
- protects the worker from dirt and from contamination from the items handled
- avoids contamination passing from the worker to the food or clean area
- colour usually khaki, grey, navy or dark green
(*See* photograph on p. 32.)

Fabric	*Care and maintenance*
cotton/terylene mix	frequent soak, warm wash, cool rinse, drip dry

Shoes or boots
(male/female)
- for full protection from heavy weights, heat and grease

Care and maintenance
regular cleaning and repair

Hygiene

A good standard of personal hygiene is of great importance to all staff working in the food production, food service, accommodation and cleaning and maintenance sections of the catering industry.

It gives a feeling of freshness, health and well-being to staff who work close to customers. A clean appearance shows that the worker is careful not only about personal hygiene but also food hygiene and cleaning standards. It makes the customer confident that all areas of the work are being hygienically taken care of.

Good health is essential for staff who are working long hours in tiring conditions and the achievement of high standards of personal hygiene will assist in the maintenance of health.

Adequate sleep, fresh air, exercise and suitable diet will also contribute to this.

Personal hygiene

The body

Danger	*Care*
• heat exhaustion due to build up of perspiration	wash and shower regularly
• offensive body odour from stale perspiration	change underwear and workwear daily, wear loose clothing, drink adequate amounts of water, eat regular, light meals

Cuts

Danger	*Care*
• food contamination passed from cuts to food in process of preparation	use correct first aid materials
• cross infection in the cleaning situation	cover all cuts, boils, sores and infected areas: use waterproof material, change dressings regularly

Colds

Danger	*Care*
• contamination of food due to sneezing or germs passed from nose to hands to food through the need to wipe nose regularly	stay away from food or cleaning operations at the height of the cold, move out of the production or cleaning area to the cloakroom for nose wiping and then wash your hands, use disposable tissues and dispose of them into a polythene bag and then into an outside waste bin or incinerator
• germs sprayed from the mouth through coughing	cover mouth with disposable tissue when coughing: wash hands

Hair

Danger
- scurf and hair falling into food or onto newly cleaned and prepared surfaces
- hair becoming grease-laden due to the kitchen atmosphere or dry due to air conditioning

Care
tie or pin hair well back, cover hair completely with a net, hat or scarf

wash hair regularly in a suitable shampoo, keep hair well covered to protect it from dirt, dust, steam and heat

Hands

Danger
- hands can pass contamination from one food item to another during preparation
- hands also pass contamination from all parts of the worker's body and clothing to the food or newly cleaned surface
- used in smoking hands transfer germs from the mouth to the working area or food item being prepared

Care
follow the handwashing code: always wash your hands
(a) each time you enter the work area
(b) after smoking
(c) after nose blowing or sneezing
(d) after touching spots or cuts
(e) before and between each food preparation or cleaning operation
(f) after visiting the toilet
(g) after handling dirty store and stock items and chemical cleaning agents

- nails harbour germs under the tip. These can be transferred to food or cleaning particularly when the dirt is softened by water (e.g. in the washing-up sink or general cleaning situation)

keep nails short, well manicured and clean
use the nail brush and soap provided each time you wash your hands

Feet

Danger
- feet can become tired, swollen and aching in the practical working situation due to heat, synthetic carpets, poor floor surfaces, and long periods of standing still

Care
wash feet regularly, change shoes often, wear leather shoes to allow feet to breathe (avoid synthetic materials) never stand in one place too long (move gently from foot to foot), notice heat building up and ventilate the working area as necessary

Sickness

Danger
- sickness on its own or with diarrhoea can be a source of

Care
all bouts of sickness and diarrhoea must be reported to the supervisor

food poisoning bacteria which may contaminate food or cleaning operations that the sick worker is involved in

- sickness can lead to lack of concentration and possible danger

- fainting and dizziness can result in the worker hitting a piece of large equipment and hurting themselves or others in the process

- skin irritation may harbour damaging bacteria and may be made worse by use of, for example, water, flour, cleaning agents and detergents

- infectious diseases can cause contamination of food, clean areas, and fellow workers

immediately, greater care must be taken with all usual hygiene safeguards, e.g. hand washing and toilet care

be aware that you are slightly 'under the weather': move slowly, think carefully and avoid really heavy work

as soon as there is warning of faintness or dizziness, sit down in a breezy or cool place, away from the work area, keep calm and breathe deeply; place head between knees

wear protective creams, gloves, arm and eye coverings as provided, avoid handling the items which cause irritation, wash affected area well after handling the items which cause irritation, consult your doctor

any contact with infectious diseases must be reported immediately to the supervisor

Teeth

Danger

- bad teeth will cause general ill-health and will harbour bacteria which may be spread through talking, coughing and sneezing onto food or clean surfaces

Care

have regular dental checks, clean teeth thoroughly and regularly

Toilet care

Danger

- food poisoning bacteria can be transferred from the body to uniform, door handles, food and clean surfaces following a visit to the toilet

Care

wash hands after visiting the toilet and before leaving the cloakroom area, remove top items of work wear before using the toilet, never use the toilet cubicle as a smoking or rest area

Health and safety

The Health and Safety at Work Act (1974) lays down rules of behaviour and the conditions which must exist in the working place to make it safe for workers, visitors and customers.

The employer is responsible for providing and maintaining safe working conditions and for training staff to use safe and hygienic working methods.

The worker takes responsibility for his/her own safe and hygienic conduct and works for the safety of others in the immediate working area. The worker agrees to use all the safety procedures laid down by the employer and take part in training for accident prevention, fire prevention, hazard spotting and emergency procedures.

The employer and employee jointly share responsibility for safety and must co-operate together to achieve this.

A copy of the company Health and Safety Policy must be available for all staff to read.

A public notice explaining the accident reporting procedure must be placed in a prominent position in the working area.

Any dangerous piece of equipment or danger area will be clearly marked with warning labels.

Accident prevention

Accidents can be prevented by using the correct process for each job, by spotting any hazard which may cause danger and by behaving in a sensible and thoughtful manner.

Accident prevention behaviour

1   Avoid being overtired.
2   Concentrate at all times.
3   Don't rush or run – keep calm and controlled.
4   Don't make too much noise or distract the attention of other workers by shouting.
5   Never take part in horseplay, practical jokes, fights or arguments.
6   Use equipment only when authorised and trained.
7   Use methods as instructed.
8   Use safety procedures at all times.
9   Wear uniform correctly – button sleeves and tuck in ties.
10   Wear correct shoes.

Hazards to spot

Any hazard spotted should be reported to the supervisor immediately.

Cutting blades

Hazard	Prevention
• using blunt knives	keep knives regularly sharpened
• handling knives carelessly or incorrectly	use the knives as instructed, never play about with them
• placing knives in the washing-up sink	always wash sharp knives yourself as soon as possible after use and never put them in a sink of water
• storing knives loosely and without protection	always guard knives with a sheath or in a wooden box or attach to a wall clip when not in use

- using unguarded cutting blades on the gravity feed food slicer or bread slicer
- using unguarded blades on the vegetable chopper or clipper

always use the safety guard as instructed: remember that you are responsible for your own safety as above

Electricity
Hazard

Prevention

- cleaning electrical appliances and equipment with water while electric current is flowing
- using equipment with wet hands

- trailing flexes

- badly wired or damaged plugs

- exposed or faulty wiring

before starting to clean any powered item switch off at the equipment wall switch
never use electrical equipment with wet hands and so avoid the risk of a shock
use a flex roll where possible to hold long flexes in position, or place a 'working' sign by the flex
report the damage and mark the item not to be used; never attempt to repair it yourself
as above

Heat
Hazard

Prevention

- incorrect handling of hot items being removed from burners or oven
- careless handling of pans full of hot food
- using damp or inadequate oven cloths

always use two dry cloths – one in each hand

always use two dry cloths – one in each hand
always use two dry cloths – one in each hand

Obstacles
Hazard

Prevention

- mops and buckets left lying in main traffic routes
- any item which is out of its normal position
- damaged floor surfaces, e.g. cracked tiles
- unmarked areas where workmen are undertaking alterations or repairs

mark any area where periodic or unusual work is being done
mark any area where periodic or unusual work is being done
report damage

mark the area

Spillage
Hazard

Prevention

- fresh spillage of any food or liquid on the floor which will cause slipping
- old spillage which may dry on the floor causing it to be sticky

clear spillage immediately

do thorough, regular and correct cleaning

- spilt food which will provide a suitable place for bacteria to develop

do thorough, regular and correct cleaning

Stacked goods

Hazard

- items not stacked on a sound base
- goods haphazardly piled

- items stacked against exit doors or in gangways

- items stacked in busy areas

Prevention

stack firm heavy items at the base of a large stack
keep all piles and stacks neat and in order
never block exit doors or gangways: this causes a great hazard in the event of fire
avoid bringing unnecessary items into the working area

Weight/heavy equipment

Hazard

- lifting items which are too heavy
- moving items which are too heavy
- moving too quickly when carrying heavy goods

- not using correct body posture when lifting

Prevention

use mechanical lifting aids where possible or ask for help
as above: make sure you use the correct technique and *never* strain
move slowly and carefully to avoid strain and the danger of bumping into other people
always bend your knees and keep back straight when lifting goods: ask for instructions in lifting technique

Reporting an accident

Any accident, large or small which occurs in the working area must be reported immediately to the supervisor. Details of the accident will be recorded in an accident book or on an accident form. The detail will cover:

- the name of the person injured
- the place where the accident happened
- what happened
- how badly injured the worker was
- what first aid was given
- what further treatment was given e.g. sent to local hospital
- was the worker doing a job he/she was expected to do?
- who was supervising at the time?
- were there any witnesses?
- the exact date and time that the accident occurred

The record which is signed by the employer and the injured person is kept by the employer in case a claim for compensation is made by the injured person at a later date.

How many hazards are in this picture?
(reproduced by permission of RoSPA — Royal Society for the Prevention of Accidents)

First aid box

> A full first aid kit must be placed in the working area to satisfy the requirements of the Health & Safety at Work Act (1974).

Contents   *Guidance card*
> gives general instruction and warning on the use of the materials in the first aid box

> *Individually wrapped sterile adhesive dressing (plasters)*
> for covering cuts and sores which otherwise would become contaminated by the work materials or would pass on contaminating agents to food or clean surfaces (adhesive dressings should be coloured)

Polythene finger stalls
to cover adhesive or sterile dressing to give protection from liquid

Sterile triangular bandage
to hold temporarily any limb which may have been damaged or broken and to act as an immediate air excluding cover in the case of burns

Medium and large sterile dressing packs
to be used on major cuts or burns

Safety pins and scissors
to assist in the cutting and securing of protective coverings which are applied to cut, burnt or broken areas
   Any first aid treatment, however simple, should be applied by the chosen person in the work unit, who has had some first aid training. Giving the incorrect treatment can be dangerous and cause later damage.

Fire equipment

Fire blanket: (100% fibreglass)
for small fires and equipment fires;
the blanket is used to cover and smother the flame and extinguish the fire by excluding the air

Fire extinguishers
warning: it is essential to use the correct extinguisher for a particular purpose; all extinguishers must be used with great care as instructed
1   red label (Water CO_2 soda acid): for fires involving paper, cloth, cardboard and textiles;
unsafe all voltages
2   blue label (dry powder): for fires involving oil, paint, petrol; safe on low voltages
3   cream label (foam): for fires involving grease, fat, petrol, oil;
unsafe all voltages
4   black label (CO_2 Carbon dioxide) fires involving live electrical apparatus; safe on high voltages
5   green label (vaporising liquid) for fires involving electrical equipment and petrol; safe on high voltages

Fire hose
for use on fires involving wood, paper, cardboard and cloth

Safety labels and symbols

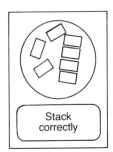

Working in a team

Most food production, food and beverage service, and cleaning and maintenance tasks are completed by organised teams. The team members share a goal and work together to achieve success for the company and for all of the team members. A team will be successful if all members fully play their part, and the rule for the successful team membership is – 'Behave to other people as you would like them to behave towards you!'

Why are workers organised into teams?

1 To allow the work to be spread out evenly and give efficient organisation and allocation of jobs.

2 To share special skills and experience and to achieve success and job satisfaction, which each member alone may not be capable of.

3 To share information and learn from each other.

4 To give support, encouragement and confidence to each other.

5 To help co-operation between staff.

6   To provide friendship, company and shared enjoyment in the working situation.
7   To get best use out of shared equipment.
8   To promote speed and efficiency.
9   To give variety and rotation of work.
10   To give security and to share the stress of pressured work situations.

What are the problems of working in a team?

1   Team members may disagree about how to do a job or the standard required, or the way the work has been allocated.
2   There may be disagreements and personality clashes.
3   Individual team members may be lazy and not carry out their fair share of work.
4   Some members may produce work of a low standard and spoil the team efforts.

Coping with problems

Whether you work as part of a team or on your own, problems will arise in the working situations.
To deal with a problem decide:
1   Exactly what the problem is.
2   Does it need an immediate answer?
3   Can you solve the problem yourself?
4   Who is the best person to help you?
Some problems and ideas for coping are given below.

Job problems

1   Too much work to do in time allowed
Ask yourself:
- are you using the best and fastest method?
- are you carrying out the work which someone else should be doing?
- are you concentrating all the time and pre-planning your work, or do you let your mind wander and lose attention, or allow yourself to be distracted by others?

Act:
- rethink the way you do each job
- ask the supervisor to re-examine your work load or suggest a new way of working
- concentrate fully on your work.

2   Too little work to fill the time allocated
Ask yourself:
- are you doing the job well enough and reaching a high enough standard?
- are you covering all the tasks in your list or are you letting other people do part of your work?

Act:
- check out your job description and work card
- give full attention to every detail and raise your standards.

3   Not enough variety of work or new things to learn: you feel that your progress is too slow
Ask yourself:
● whether the standard of work you are producing is good enough for you to be offered new and interesting work
● whether you show enough enthusiasm and willingness to take on new and varied work.

Act:
● ask for a discussion with the supervisor
● tell the supervisor that you do wish to make progress and enquire how best this can be done in the work place.

4   Not sure how to organise your work; not sure how to carry out a particular job
Ask yourself:
● how other people in the unit plan and carry out their work.

Act:
● get help from the supervisor or other workers – don't be afraid to ask
● ask the supervisor for a written work plan which includes some idea of how long each job should take and the best order to carry out the jobs
● ask for more on-the-job training.

5   Criticised for poor work; anxious about completing work on time and to the right standard
Ask yourself:
● whether you are capable of better work if you give the job your full attention
● why you are not interested enough or skilled enough to do good work
● what effect you are having on other workers by not producing good work.

Act:
● to be a full member of the team by copying the standards of the best workers
● ask for explanation and fresh instruction from the supervisor on each task that is criticised
● be prepared to think about the job and to learn
● make a real effort to do your best
● tell the supervisor about your worries.

6   Unable to work with the rest of the team
Ask yourself:
● if you are behaving in a way which others find acceptable
● whether you are doing your fair share of the work
● whether certain aspects of your behaviour are used to deliberately annoy one or more members of the group.

Act:

- to curb silly or thoughtless behaviour
- to take a fair share of the work
- to keep out of the way of individuals who annoy you
- curb your anger or too impulsive reactions.

7   Unable to work easily with the supervisor
Ask yourself:

- whether you accept that the supervisor's requests have to be followed.

Act:

- remember that the supervisor is planning for the good of the whole group and not just you
- be polite and correct in conversation and to try and understand both sides of an issue
- if you disagree with the supervisor, get the reasons clear in your mind and discuss them quietly, calmly and privately with the supervisor.

8   Wages seem to be incorrect or not the right rate for the job
Ask yourself:

- what wage rate was agreed in your contract?

Act:

- ask the supervisor to check the details on your pay slip and the rate agreed for your work
- check the number of hours worked.

9   Working too many extra hours – with or without extra pay
Ask yourself:

- whether you need to do these extra hours. Are you working too slowly or staying on duty after your real work is over?

Act:

- work hard in the time allowed and complete your work within the basic hours
- don't feel that you have to accept regular overtime with or without pay, but be flexible in an emergency
- discuss the matter with the supervisor in relation to the hours agreed in your contract (*see* p. 25).

Personal problems

1   Generally not getting on with other workers
Ask yourself:

- why you are not getting on with them. Are you shy, quiet, noisy, thoughtless, aggravating, cheeky, interfering, standoffish, bad tempered, or generally difficult to get along with?
- whether the group is behaving in a way that you like.

Act:

- if you are difficult to get along with, try to 'play down' your worst points

- think more about the feelings of other people
- offer friendship to others, make the first move towards them
- if the behaviour of the group is not your style, and if you really can't approve of it, then don't be afraid to stick to your principles and conduct yourself according to your own standards. It may make you a bit lonely but it will eventually earn you respect.

2   Shy or lonely and finding it difficult to mix with other workers
Act:
- make the first move – smile
- listen to other workers – remember what interests them
- work out a few special things to say at the start of a conversation
- look interested and friendly
- take up any offers of friendship which other people make and be quietly 'nice to be with'
- develop an interest of your own.

3   Changes in the working pattern make it difficult to organise your private life – to join clubs or classes
Act:
- discuss the matter with the supervisor
- pick out one or two priority activities and stick with those.

4   Sickness, major or minor, is affecting your work
Act:
- have a medical check;
- live sensibly – good food and plenty of sleep and fresh air
- try to put it to the back of your mind and concentrate on work. It will cause 'ill-feeling' if you do not 'pull your weight'.

5   Unhappiness at home is making it difficult for you to concentrate on work
Act:
- try to leave home problems at home and let the enjoyment of doing a good job take over. Think about 'living in' or living with a group of friends.

3

CATERING FACILITIES –
THE TOOLS OF THE TRADE

> Catering equipment, small, medium and large
> Cleaning and maintenance
> Production flow and kitchen layout

Catering equipment

Small equipment

Care and storage　Small equipment is expensive and it is easily lost and damaged. In all cases for metal (aluminium, steel or stainless steel) plastic and wood the items should be washed immediately after use, rinsed and thoroughly dried, and replaced in a clean storage drawer or rack. Take care not to throw small utensils away with waste material. Never put items loose into a full washing-up sink as they may cause injury to staff or be damaged by heavier items.

Cooking tins　1　*Baking sheets*
Usually aluminium and a wide range of size. Should be purchased to suit a modular system, for most efficient oven use, and be a size which is suitable for easy handling.
Use: for bakery and confectionery. Use under containers large and small to act as the drip-tray and assist in the easy handling of batches of individual items.

2　*Pie dishes*
Usually aluminium: a range of shapes available. For economic oven use a modular system, e.g. Gastronorm is best. Disposable foil containers are suitable for freezer item preparation and for individual small items.
Use: for all baking uses: for savoury and sweet pies or stewed items.

3　*Pudding sleeves*
Aluminium cylinders 16–20 portion size.
Use: for steamed sweets and savoury items, e.g. suet mince roll.

4　*Roasting tins*
Wrought steel or aluminium roasting tins do not have a lid. Gastronorm multipurpose containers can be used for roasting.
Use: for open oven roast. Tin foil covering can be used to protect the meat. Gastronorm containers can have a lid and be used also for oven stewing and braising.

Kitchen knives

Boning knife

Cook's knife (vegetable)

1 Boning knife
The shaped blade makes the knife manoeuvrable around the meat bone. The carbon steel blade must be regularly sharpened.
Use: for all boning purposes for raw or cooked meat.

2 Cook's knife
4" or 6" [103 mm or 155 mm] (vegetable knife)
Small shaped handle or short carbon steel blade or stainless steel blade.
Use: for fine preparation and vegetable paring and finishing.

3 Cook's knife
8" (205 mm)
A general purpose preparation and chopping knife. Cook's knives are also available with longer and heavier blades 10", 12" (255 mm, 305 mm). Usually carbon steel, can be stainless steel.
Use: for all preparation and chopping use. The knife is rocked using the whole length of the blade for effective chopping.

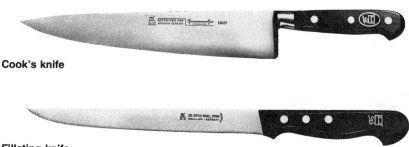

Cook's knife

Filleting knife

4 Filleting knife
A long flexible carbon steel or stainless steel blade. 6" (155 mm) blade.
Use: for skinning and filleting fish.

5 Palette knife
Carbon steel or stainless steel blades 6", 8", 10", 12" (155 mm, 205 mm, 255 mm, 305 mm) blades.
Use: for moving prepared food items; for turning cooked items; for lifting cooked items from oven trays.

6 Steel
A carbon steel bar with wooden or polypropylene handle.

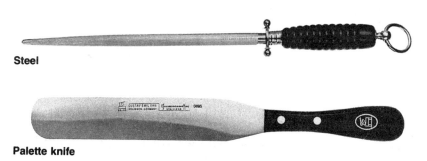

Steel

Palette knife

Use: for sharpening all steel knives. These may also be sharpened on an abrasive block or powered knife sharpener.

Note: Steel knives: it is possible to achieve a very sharp edge on steel knives, but they need to be sharpened regularly between each use. Stainless.steel: it is not possible to get such a high degree of sharpness, but the sharpness is retained over a long period.

Kitchen tools

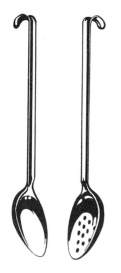

1   *Ladle – service*
Stainless steel
Use: for portioning raw food into cooking containers and cooked food into service containers

2   *Ladle – perforated*
Stainless steel
Use: for draining cooked items and measuring portions into service containers. Ladle size should match required portion size.

3   *Spoon – service*
Stainless steel
Use: as for service ladle.

4   *Spoon – perforated*
Stainless steel
Use: as for perforated ladle.

5   *Spoons and spatulas – wood*
Either spoon-shaped or flat. A whole range of sizes from spoons: 10″ – 18″ (255 mm–455 mm); spatulas 10″–48″ (255 mm–1220 mm).
Use: for mixing and stirring a wide range of food items in small or bulk production processes. All wooden items must be dried out thoroughly after washing.

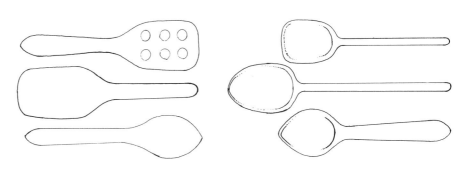

6   *Rotary or balloon whisk*
Stainless steel or tinned piano wire.
Use: for heavy whisking or light whisking in large quantities, e.g. egg or batter.

7   *Flat whisk*
As above.
Use: for light whisking of small quantities.

Rotary whisk

Flat whisk

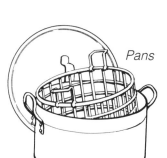

Friture

Omelette pan

Sauté pan

Stockpot

Pans

1   *Boiling pan*
Double handled aluminium with lid. Wide range of size capacity:
2 litres – 65 litres
4 pints – 116 pints
Use: top stove or oven use for all boiling and stewing operations.

2   *Braising pan*
As above but shallower.
Capacity 19–53 pints
               11–30 litres
Use: top braising vegetables and main meal items.

3   *Frying pan*
Single or double-handled shallow pan. Cast aluminium. Size range
10″–17″ (255 mm–432 mm).
Use: for all shallow frying purposes. Large oval shape used for large quantities.

4   *Friture*
Round or oval. Single or double handled. Has a wire basket lining.
Aluminium size range 9″–22″ (230 mm–558 mm).
Use: for all deep fat frying uses. For small quantity batch frying.

5   *Omelette pan*
Aluminium, copper or wrought steel. A shallow, round, single handled pan. Size range 6″–12″, 152 mm–304 mm.
Use: for omelettes and crepes, (pancakes) only.

6   *Sauté pan*
A long handled shallow pan. Aluminium 12″–14″ (305 mm–355 mm) in diameter.
Use: top stove use only.

7   *Stew pan/saucepan*
(*a*) Single-handled aluminium with lid.
(*b*) Double handled with lid.
Capacity range: 4–12 pints, 2–7 litres.
Use: (*a*) top stove use only, (*b*) top stove or oven use. For all boiling and stewing operations.

8   *Stockpot*
A deep, lidded pan with tap near to the base for 'letting off' stock.
Double handled. Aluminium – heavy duty.
Use: top stove use only. For large batch stock making.

Portion aids 1 *Measuring spoons and ladles*
Stainless steel portion sized spoons and ladles.
Use: assist in portion control. The ladle or spoon size must match the size of the calculated service portion.

2 *Servers*
Aluminium or stainless steel flan server and pie server
Use: aid to hygienic food handling. Helps to achieve portion control by preventing portion loss through damage to food.

3 *Scoops*
Stainless steel chip scoop: perforated/or solid. Stainless steel vegetable scoop. Ice cream scoop.
Use: portion aids. The scoop size should match the required portion size. A wide range of sizes available.

4 *Tongs*
Aluminium. General purpose food handling tongs
Fish tongs.
Plastic tongs for pastry and confectionery.
Use: aid to hygienic food handling. Allows the food handler to move food without touching it.

Medium equipment

Food processing 1 *Cutter mixer*
A single chamber all-purpose machine. Used for quick action bulk-preparation. Bowl capacity – 30 or 45 litres.
Use: for bulk processing: mixing cakes and pastry, chopping meat and vegetables, kneading, i.e. dough

2 *Bowl/chopper* (*food cutter*)
A rotating bowl brings the food in contact with the cutting blades. For coarse cutting use short time, for fine cutting use longer time.

Cutter mixer

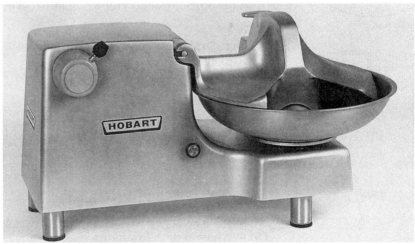

Food cutter

Use: for meat and vegetable chopping, e.g. for stews and paté. Cuts salad items. With attachments can mince, dice, chip, shred and grate.

3   Gravity feed food slicer
There is an adjustable thickness gauge. A sharpener is built into the machine and the blade is stainless steel. Some models have 2 speed automatic slicing. All machines can be taken apart easily for regular cleaning.
Use: a general purpose food slicing machine. Used mainly for hot and cold boned meat. It cuts evenly quickly and economically. The machine must be thoroughly washed between each type of use. Safety guards must be in place when the machine is in use.

Mincer

4   Mincer
An independent power unit drives the mince shaft blades. Front plates can be used for coarse or fine mince.
Use: for mincing raw or cooked meat. To produce vegetable puree or breadcrumbs.

5   Mixer and attachments
Small heavy duty mixers can be obtained with capacity as little as 4.5 litres. Bulk mixers have a size range from Bench models with 12 litre capacity bowl to floor model with 92 litre bowl-capacity. The machine has a speed gear change (usually 3 speeds) and is supplied with basic whisk, hook and beater attachments. Mixers usually have stainless steel bowls and stove enamel body.
Use: for general purpose mixing, beating and whisking of large batches of food. With additional attachments can mince, dice, shred and grate.

Mixer

6   Food processor robot
A single chamber all-purpose machine. Bowl capacity 2 or 4 litres, (will mix up to 4lb of pastry)
Use: mixing cakes and pastries; chopping meat and vegetables; kneading dough; liquidising fruit, vegetables, paté; grating cheese and vegetables.

7   Potato chipper/slicer
An independent power unit drives the chipper. Performance 14–18 kg (30–40 lbs) per minute.
Use: for cutting chips. 4 size cutters are available. Chips can also be cut on the all-purpose machines or with a hand-chipper.

8   Potato peeler
An independent power unit drives the peeler. A constant flow of water washes the peelings away through a trap and into a drain outlet.
Capacity range:

7 lb	14 lb	28 lb	56 lb
3.5 kg	7 kg	12 kg	25 kg

Potato chipper

Use: for peeling potatoes and root vegetables.

Large equipment – food production

Fryers   *1   Computer controlled*
As for rapid recovery, computer control can be built into the fryer or a control mechanism attached to the fryer.

Rapid recovery fryer

Use: computer control gives standard temperature and time control automatically for each batch of food. Temperature and timings will be varied to suit each different type of food.

2　Rapid recovery
Made of stainless steel, a quick recovery, single-pan fryer has the capacity to cook 35 lb of chips per hour. With a large double basket pan the capacity can be enlarged to 120 lbs chips per hour. The fryers are thermostatically controlled. Table models are used for back-bar. Portion-mat automatic chip fryers and dispensers are used in fast food operations.
Use: all deep frying of fish, meat, fritters and chips. The rapid recovery makes them particularly suitable for frying frozen food items. The oil must be filtered and cleaned regularly.

3　Fry plate/griddle
This solid metal plate is pre-heated and lightly greased. Food is placed directly on it for fast cooking. Can be heated by gas or electricity.
Use: used as part of fast finish or back-bar operations for all shallow frying, eggs, steaks, burgers, bacon, etc.

Grills　*1　Grill, top heat*
Can be bench mounted or wall mounted. The stainless steel, aluminium or enamelled cabinet has moveable grill rack. The heating element is usually divided into two to allow for economic use. Grills can be heated by gas or electricity.
Use: for general purpose grilling of meat, fish, toast and for browning items, e.g. meringue, and cheese-topped foods.

2　Infra-red grills
As above, but fast-cooking and energy-saving with the heat evenly distributed.
Use: as above.

Top-heat grill

Chargrill

Rotary toaster

3   Chargrill/charbroiler
Gas or electrically heated, the chargrill grid is used directly for holding food. It can be angled to vary the effect of the heat. Refractory stones produce the same effect and flavour as charcoal.
Use: used for meat, e.g. steaks, sausages, burgers and for fish. Automatic conveyor broilers are used for burgers and buns in fast food operations.

4   Rotary toaster
Slices of bread are placed directly on a conveyor belt and are carried through the toaster until brown.
Capacity – 450 slices of toast per hour.
Use: for bulk toast production where demand is high and continuous.

Ovens   *1   Barbecue oven – spit roast*
A specialised rotary spit oven, often with see-through casing for point of sale cookery. Usually stainless steel or enamel. Counter models are available.
Average capacity 6–25 chickens
15–60 lbs meat.
Use: for counter cooking and service of meat. Chicken and pressed meat items.

Microwave

Pizza oven (by courtesy of Zanussi)

2   Baking oven/pastry oven
Single, double or treble tier. Usually made of cast iron, sheet steel with stainless steel outer finish. May have tiled oven base. Will take standard bake trays. Top and bottom heat control. Gas or electrically heated.
Use: the single shallow shelf gives ideal conditions for cooking and browning all bakery and confectionery products, e.g. bread, cakes, biscuits, pastries and pies.

3   Convection – forced air circulation
The natural convection action is fan assisted to drive the heat evenly through the oven cabinet. This ensures even cooking and allows the oven to be fully loaded without losing any efficiency. Some models have a cook/hold facility. Others have a roll in loading rack.
Use: for all cooking purposes. It gives even cooking and is quicker and more efficient than conventional gas or electric oven cooking. Table models can be used as part of back-bar operations.

4   Convection/steam or water injection
These combination ovens are basically convection ovens with the addition of humidifier, water or steam to moisten the products, e.g. baked items.
Use: used as for convection oven, but the addition of moisture makes them very suitable for baking. Can be used in place of bakers' ovens.

5   Microwave
The microwave oven cooks or re-heats food rapidly. Radio waves jostle the molecules of the food and so transmit heat. Microwaves do not brown food or assist in the development of flavour. Automatic controls time the heating process. Timings should be carefully controlled.
Use: Primarily used for fast finish foods, the re-heating of pre-prepared individual items, snacks, mains, sweets, and drinks. Widely and safely used for defrosting frozen food.

6   Microwave/browner
As above, but with browning facility.
Use: As above.

7   Microwave/convection
A combination of microwave power and forced air convection. The microaire oven is more of a prime cooker than the microwave oven. Metal items can be used in it.
Use: can roast, bake, braise or poach. For larger quantity fast cooking and finishing. Also used in back-bar and fast food operations.

8   Pizza oven
Multi deck pizza ovens have rapid recovery facility for constant, heavy use. Each deck has separate thermostatic control. Stainless steel counter top models are available.
Use: multi deck ovens are used for large quantity specialised pizza production. The small ovens can be used as part of back bar operations.

9   Proving oven
The cabinet is equipped to take standard cooking trays, e.g. gastronorm.

The temperature and humidity are controlled at 26–28°C or 80–83°F. Can be gas or electrically heated with automatic water fill.
Use: used in the proving of yeast goods in warm moist conditions.

10   Range – electric
A range is a combination of oven and hot plates.
Usually stainless steel or enamelled.Oven and plates are thermostatically temperature controlled.
Oven doors are well-insulated and heavy and may open downwards or outwards.
Use: general purpose baking, braising, roasting oven. Top plates used for boiling, poaching, shallow frying.

Electric range

11   Range – gas
A combination of oven and top burners or solid top plates (usually stainless steel or enamelled). Ovens are temperature controlled at each gas mark setting. Burners are usually manually controlled.
Use: as above. The solid top can be temperature-controlled but pans are usually moved from the centre hot area to the side, cooler areas to vary the cooking temperature.

12   Roasting oven – slow
Slow roasting can be done in a cook-hold convection oven or a slow roast oven. The slow roast oven operates on low temperature cooking so avoiding shrinkage, drying and weight loss. The oven can be used overnight or in off-peak hours for greater saving. The minimum allowable holding temperature is 150°F or 66°F.
Use: the oven saves on both fuel and weight loss and retains the flavour of the meat. Used mainly for meat joints.

13　Steaming oven – atmospheric

In the well-insulated cabinet the steam is formed when water in the well is heated by gas or electricity. The water that is driven off as steam is constantly replaced by an automatically controlled supply of water. A direct source of steam can also be used. Usually made of stainless steel, the racks are removable.

Use: used for bulk steaming of meat, fish, vegetables and puddings. Great care should be taken when opening the door or removing trays to avoid direct contact with an outrush of steam or drips of boiling water.

14　Steamer/rotopan

The rotopan operates like the steaming oven. It is made up of three separate, hinged, moveable layers, all heated from steam in the rotopan well.

Use: the three layers allow for smaller quantities of different foods to be steamed at the same time.

15　Pressure steamer

The water is heated in a well in the steamer compartment and used under pressure to speed up the cooking process.

Note: doors must not be opened until all pressure has been released from the cabinet. Always follow manufacturers' instructions.

Pressure steamer (by courtesy of Zanussi)

Use: used with small models as part of fast finish or back-bar operation for small batches of food. With larger models to deliver quickly a constant supply of vegetables, puddings, e.g. as 'back-up' to Ganymede service.

16 Pressureless steamer (convector steamer)
The pressureless/convection steamer is very swift and can incorporate a controlled defrost facility. It cooks with steam only and the convection system removes air constantly from the chamber. This makes the steaming action more efficient and retains the flavour of the food.
Use: used for fast-finish operations where quick defrost and heat of pre-prepared dishes or raw frozen items is required. Can also be used for quick batch heating and back-up to heavy demand cafeteria service or Gannymede.

Pressureless steamer (by courtesy of Zanussi)

Pans 1 *Bain marie*
A bain marie is a heated water bath. Stainless steel containers with lids rest in a bath of water which can be heated by electricity, gas or a direct steam source.
Use: for the food production area for keeping food warm, e.g. sauces, or for very slow cooking, e.g. custards. In the service area for holding food on cafeteria service counter or by the Ganymede plated service conveyor.

2 Boiling pan
A large, free-standing lidded pan with direct water filling valve and an emptying outlet. Can be direct fired or jacketed (surrounded by a water jacket for indirect heating). Capacity range from 10–20 gallons, 45–90 litres. Split pans are also available.

Bain marie (by courtesy of Zanussi)

Boiling pan (by courtesy of Zanussi)

Bratt pan (by courtesy of Zanussi)

Use: for large batch vegetable cooking, soups, stews, stock, sweet and savoury sauces, milk puddings.

3   Bratt pan
A large shallow tilting pan which is moved by the action of a wheel. Made of cast iron, steel or stainless steel. It has a hinged cover and the heat is controlled by a thermostat.
Use: a very versatile piece of equipment, the Bratt pan is used for shallow frying, poaching stewing, boiling and braising.

Refrigeration   *1   Blast chiller*
A small cabinet is used and batches of food are continuously and quickly passed through it. Capacity 20–60 kg. It can be a tunnel chiller: cooked

Blast chiller

items go in one end and chilled items come out of the other. A full load will be chilled from 65°C (150°F) to 2°C (37°F) within 1½ hrs (90 minutes). The food can be trolley loaded into the chiller as in the Regethermic system.

Use: as part of the cook/chill food preparation system. Can also be used to chill rapidly any food items which were prepared extra to need, or items to be held during preparation for later finishing.

2   Blast freezer

Blast freeze cabinets are used to freeze items for long-term storage. The temperature of the cooked food is reduced quickly to –20°C(–4°F) Capacity ranges from 11 kg (25 lb) to 400 kg (900 lbs).

Use: food is usually frozen in individual or multi-portion packs. Used for made-up meat and sweet dishes. Special recipes are required as freezing can change the nature and appearance of cooked food.

3   Chilled food storage cabinet/refrigerator

The upright refrigerator cabinet should be suitably shelved for the particular use. Cabinets are usually stainless steel or aluminium. For cook-chill a modular gastronorm shelf system can be used for maximum storage.

Use: for general food storage use. Dairy goods 3°C–6°C (38°F–42°F) Meat 0°C–2°C (32°F–36°F) Fish: – 1°C to 1°C (30°F to 34°F) Cook-chill items 3°C (38°F) (The chill cabinet as part of the cook/chill system should be used for this purpose only to maintain a constant low temperature.)

4   Deep freeze cabinet (upright or top opening)
Deep freeze cabinets cover a temperature range –21°C to –18°C (–5°F to 0°F). They should be opened as little as possible to maintain the correct degree of cold. Deep freeze cabinets should be locked to keep goods secure.
Use: for long-term storage of deep-frozen items. Cook-freeze food is usually stored at –20°C (–4°F). Foods should be labelled clearly and stacked to ensure correct stock rotation.

5   Walk-in refrigerator – cold room
Walk in cold rooms are fitted in to the fabric of the building to take on the shape of a room. Doors are heavy to ensure good insulation. There is a safety handle which can be used from the inside in case of emergency. Cold rooms can be held at general use temperature –1°C to 6°C or (30°F to 42°F) or deep freeze –21°C to –18°C (or –5°F to 0°F).
Use: for general purpose cold storage or long-term deep freeze storage.

Stores handling

1   Scales
(a) Heavy duty counter or floor scales. Capacity 200 lb/9 kg.
(b) Table scales, capacity 28 lb.
(c) Spring scales or balance weights.
Use:
(a) for sacks, cases or complete packs.
(b) for general weighing use, for small quantity.
(c) for split pack items.

2   Stacker
For hand use. The stacker is lifted by a winch.
Use: for stacking heavy packs or cans on high storage shelves.

3   Trolley
General purpose four wheel trolley with three removable shelves
Use: for the kitchen or servery area, for the movement of prepared goods or for clearing and stacking used containers.

4   Truck
Lightweight truck for hand use.
Use: for moving (a) sacks, e.g. flour, sugar,
(b) drums, e.g. cooking oil,
(c) waste sacks and bins.

Washing up

1   Dish washer – cabinet
Dirty items are stacked face downwards in the trays which are placed in the machine, over the jets and water store. The cycle is controlled to give a wash stage, a rinse stage and a sterilise stage. The tray is static throughout the time that the cycle is being completed.

Conveyor dish washer (by courtesy of Zanussi)

Use: for a small or spread demand the cabinet is efficient. Roller table on either side of the cabinet will assist in the handling of the trays. Water must be changed frequently. Detergent will be automatically fed in.

2   Dish washer-conveyor
Dirty items are stacked face down in the racks. The conveyor carries the racks along under the jets which
(*a*) pre-soak
(*b*) wash
(*c*) rinse
(*d*) sterilise.
All four stages are complete by the time the trays reach the splash cover exit of the machine.
Use: for large quantities of washing up the conveyor system speeds up the process and cuts down the amount of handling. Detergent and sterilising agent are automatically fed into the machine in controlled quantities.

3   Dish washer-flight
Plastic pegs on the flight conveyor belt hold the dirty crockery and trays as they progress through the machine. The items pass under the four sections which in turn pre-wash, wash, rinse and sterilise. Evaporation causes the crockery to be dry as it leaves the machine.
Use: as with all machines it is most important that the wash and rinse temperatures are maintained. The flight system is used for very large quantities of washing up, e.g. central wash up for the Ganymede system; stacking and handling are kept to a minimum.

4   Glass washer
Cabinet models for specialised glass cleaning usually have an auto-

Glass washer (by courtesy of Zanussi)

matic programme of wash, rinse, sterilise, (90°C) or cold rinse. Capacity ranges from 400 items an hour to 1000 items an hour.

Use: for tumblers, wine and spirit glasses and pub glasses.

5 Pan wash (cabinet)

The heavy duty cabinet takes the upturned cooking pots and pans which are cleaned by the force of heavy water jets. Cleaning agent and sterilent is automatically fed into the pan wash cabinet.

Use: for cleaning kitchen tools, equipment used during food preparation. The timing cycle can be adjusted according to the degree of soiling. Some pre-cleaning will be necessary, for greasy or burnt items.

Waste disposal *1 Compactor*

Heavy waste is collected in the compactor cabinet. It is then crushed by a heavy weight to one fifth of its original size. The waste is bagged and stored until removed.

Use: best used for cans, cartons, bones, and other dry, heavy, waste material.

2 Waste disposal unit

Designed to stand alone or be fitted into tabling in the kitchen area or wash-up. The motor turns blades which chew up' the waste. The silt is then washed away by the constant flow of water.

Use:

For: food preparation waste, plate waste and any wet waste.

Large equipment – food finishing and service

1   Back-bar unit

Usually made up of griddle, small bain marie, table top fryer, microwave and grill.

Use: this combination of small, versatile, fast recovery equipment can be assembled to suit a particular need or the amount of space available. Used for all fast finish food purposes, in bars, cafes, and clubs.

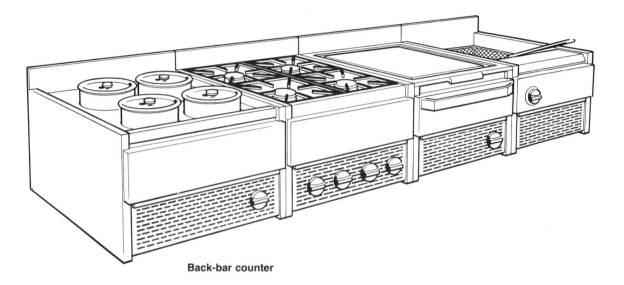

Back-bar counter

2   Conveyor plated food service, e.g. Ganymede

A central conveyor belt carries individual food trays along past the service staff who stand by heated bain maries and serve the required portion onto each plate that passes. The plates are individually heated and are transported in unheated trolleys to the satellite eating points. The system is made up of conveyor, movable bain maries, and plate lowerator holders – heated or cold. Unheated trolleys.

Use: mainly in large hospitals for central plate service, where individual meal choice is offered. Plating is carried out in the production area. All dirty items are returned to the central 'wash-up' in the production area for cleaning and storage.

3   Regethermic system regeneration equipment

The regethermic system is a cook/chill system. Food is prepared centrally, chilled, held and transported for a controlled length of time at 3°C or 38°F. Food is regenerated (re-heated), at point of eating, in the regeneration oven which uses infra-red elements. Table models are available for small-scale end use.

Use: rege loader: racks of pre-prepared chilled food are wheeled directly into the ovens and the complete meals are then re-heated for immediate service. Multi-portion trays are used for speedy banqueting service. All containers are designed to be part of the system and module sizes co-ordinate for most efficient use of space.

4 Vending equipment

Vending machines are dispensing machines which assist in the service of food. Use particularly where demand is variable and spread over a long period or to supplement other forms of service, e.g. coffee machines in cafeteria system. For off-peak or night use chill or freeze and micro-wave vend systems are available for diner operation. Cooking times are coded onto the food.

Use: for diner self-service. Hot food, cold food, snacks and drinks can be held in separate vending machines until the individual diner requires them. Hot food machines require careful temperature control of food placed in them to avoid bacterial development.

Cleaning and maintenance

Cleaning

Cleaning is carried out in order to:
1 Remove dirt, dust, grit, fats, oil, grease, food waste, litter, spillage and stains.
2 Make a work or public area pleasant for customers and staff to use.
3 Satisfy Health & Safety requirements.
4 Prevent an unacceptable build-up of dirt and soiling.
5 Prevent the growth of harmful bacteria and cross contamination.
6 Prevent accidents caused by spillage.
7 Reduce the damage and deterioration of equipment which may be harmed by an accumulation of dirt inside or on the surface.

Cleaning frequency

Cleaning is carried out:
1 Immediately after spillage or at the point of maximum need, e.g. just after use or at the end of a production or service period.
2 Daily.
3 Periodically – special or deep clean.
4 As scheduled.
It will be undertaken when the area is reasonably empty to avoid danger and inconvenience to staff and customers.

The cleaning process grid can be applied to all areas and locations of cloakroom, bar, kitchen, servery, stores, bedroom, corridors and lifts.

Cleaning process

Cleaning agents

Cleaning agents are used along with *cleaning equipment* and *cleaning materials* to achieve the required standard of hygiene and cleanliness. The cleaning agents act to:
1 Loosen, dissolve, suspend, and move dirt, grease and harmful bacteria.
2 To rinse effectively.
3 To sterilize and protect newly cleaned surfaces and areas.
Note: It is most important in the interests of safety and efficiency to select the correct cleaning agent for a particular job, to use the correct dilution and *not* to mix cleaning agents in use.

Agents are designed for a specific purpose and can cause damage or injury if improperly used.

Some multi-purpose agents are manufactured and are suitable for use as instructed on the container.

1 Abrasive cleaners
- Pumice powder (coarse)/chalk (fine)
  For enamel, porcelain, formica. These agents remove dirt by rubbing the fine particles of powder continuously against the surface being cleaned. This action can eventually damage the surface.
- *Metal polish*
  For all badly tarnished or scratched metal. Should be used as infrequently as possible. Too much polishing wears the surface away.

Cleaning Agents	Floors			Furniture & Fittings				Walls		Frequency		Soilage	
	–	–	–	Fabric	Plastic /glass	Metal	Wood	–	–	Daily	Weekly	Light	Heavy
	Terrazzo: Quarry Tiles	Wood Vinyl	Carpet	Curtains Upholstery	Windows Mirrors Fittings	Fittings Surfaces	Furniture	Paint Tiles Formica Washable Wall-paper	Fabric Wall-paper				
Pumice powder	√					√		√			√		√
Metal polish						√					√		√

2 Detergents

Detergents are cleaning agents which when added to water act to:

(a) wet the surface effectively

(b) break up soil from the surface

(c) suspend soil particles, allowing them to be carried away.

The main feature of any detergent is the surface acting agent which gives it its thorough wetting quality.

Detergents can range from neutral to alkali on the PH scale and are selected according to use.

Neutral detergents are generally not harmful on cleaned areas. The more alkaline detergents can harm skin or cleaned areas or fabrics if used carelessly.

- Alkaline or hard surface liquid detergents
  For:
  (a) cleaning heavily soiled surfaces
  (b) removing water based polishes
  need thorough rinsing and very careful handling.
- Bactericidal detergents
  For:
  (a) general kitchen cleaning
  (b) servery

(c) bar

(d) cloakroom.

Correct for use in all food handling situations.

- Buffable detergents

  For preparing and maintaining floors. Removes dirt and assists in the achievement of a gloss finish.

- Carpet and upholstery cleaners

  For use on carpets, and upholstery where shampooing is required.

- Gel cleaners

  For floor maintenance: can be buffed to give a high gloss finish.

- Laundry powders

  For laundering of fabric. Can have a soap or synthetic base. Rinse thoroughly to avoid residue. Use low foam powder for automatic machines.

- Low foam powders

  For:

  (a) dish washers

  (b) very soiled hard surfaces.

  Rinse cleaned area and hands very well after use.

Detergents	Floors			Furniture & Fittings				Walls		Frequency		Soilage	
	–	–	–	Fabric	Plastic /glass	Metal	Wood	–	–	Daily	Weekly	Light	Heavy
	Terrazzo: Quarry Tiles	Wood Vinyl	Carpet	Curtains Upholstery	Windows Mirrors Fittings	Fittings Surfaces	Furniture	Paint Tiles Formica Washable Wall-paper	Fabric Wall-paper				
Alkaline detergents	√	√				√					√		√
Bacterial detergents	√	√			√	√		√		√		√	
Buffable detergents		√									√	√	
Carpet & upholstery cleaners			√	√							Periodic	√	
Gel cleaners	√	√									√	√	
Laundry powder				√							Periodic	√	√
Low foam powders						√					Dish washers		√
Neutral detergents	√	√			√	√		√			Dish washers	√	
Multi-purpose cleansers	√	√			√	√		√			√	√	√
Toilet soap											as required	√	

- Neutral detergents
  For:
  - (a) dish washing
  - (b) general cleaning of hard surfaces.
  These are usually in liquid form and are gentle on the skin.
- Multi-purpose cleansers
  For general cleaning use on any hard surface.
- Toilet soap
  For hand and body washing in solid bar form.

3   De-greasants

These are alkaline and usually based in chemicals such as caustic soda. For cleaning any area where there is a heavy build up of fat, grease and oil, e.g. kitchen canopies, drain channels, area around fryer or cooker. *Caution*   Protective clothing must be worn. It is better to avoid a heavy build up of grease and to cut out the need to use such strong cleaning agents on a regular basis.

4   Disinfectants

For:
- (a) use in food preparation areas
- (b) cleaning and protection in cloakrooms and toilets
- (c) any area where it is necessary to safeguard against harmful micro-organisms. It is necessary to check whether a particular manufactured product is safe for use near food.

5   Polishes

Polishes are wax-based with the addition of silicone and solvents (white spirit or water). It is the proportion and type of additions which make the polish suitable for heavy duty or light duty work. The silicone gives the easy shine and greater protection to the surface.
- Cream wax
  For all types of furniture. Creams are easy to use and apply, and may be used with a damp cloth. They have some cleaning action as well as giving a gloss finish.
- Liquid polish
  For
  - (a) use for all surfaces, particularly good in food service areas and bars where staining may have occurred
  - (b) used with machine for large floor areas.
- Paste wax
  For:
  - (a) old furniture
  - (b) floors
  In both cases the shine will be dependent on regular layers of wax being added to the wood surface.
- Spray polish
  For:
  - (a) all dusty, glass, ceramic surfaces
  - (b) use with machines for large floor areas.

	Floors			Furniture & Fittings				Walls		Frequency		Soilage	
	–	–	–	*Fabric*	*Plastic /glass*	*Metal*	*Wood*	–	–	*Daily*	*Weekly*	*Light*	*Heavy*
	Terrazzo: Quarry Tiles	*Wood Vinyl*	*Carpet*	*Curtains Upholstery*	*Windows Mirrors Fittings*	*Fittings Surfaces*	*Furniture*	*Paint Tiles Formica Washable Wall-paper*	*Fabric Wall-paper*				
De-greasants						Kitchen Servery					√		√
Disinfectants	√					√		√		√	√	√	
Polishes, i.e: cream wax							√			√		√	
liquid polish		√				Servery Bar	√	√		√	√	√	√
paste wax		√					√			√	√	√	√
spray polish		√			√	Servery Bar	√					√	

6 Protective seals/finishes

For:

(*a*) wood floors

(*b*) furniture.

They protect the surfaces, restore badly worn surfaces and assist in maintenance.

7 Water

This is the simplest of all cleaning agents. It dissolves dirt, suspends it and carries it away, but on its own does not clean a surface thoroughly. Water can be used under pressure to make it more penetrating. It is most effective in moving dirt when another agent is added to it, e.g. a detergent.

Equipment 1 Brushes

- Hand brushes used for manual operations such as brushing floors where hard bristles are required, or upholstery where soft bristles

Equipment	Floors			Furniture & Fittings				Walls		Frequency		Soilage	
	–	–	–	Fabric	Plastic /glass	Metal	Wood	–	–	Daily	Weekly	Light	Heavy
	Terrazzo: Quarry Tiles	Wood Vinyl	Carpet	Curtains Upholstery	Windows Mirrors Fittings	Fittings Surfaces	Furniture	Paint Tiles Formica Washable Wall-paper	Fabric Wall-paper				
Hand brushes	√	√		√			√			√	√	√	
Roto-brushes	√	√				√		√		√	√	√	√
Power sweepers	√	√								√	√	√	√
Flat mops (dry)	√	√			√	√			√	√	√	√	
Vee mops (dry)	√	√								√		√	
Dusting mops (dry)						√			√		√	√	
Wet mops	√							√			√	√	

are required. Brushing removes dirt but is inefficient and unsatisfactory where dust control is important.
- Roto-brushes (mechanical) can be used to wet clean or dry clean high wall or ceiling areas. Interchangeable hard and soft brush heads.
- Power sweepers (mechanical) offer a combined brush/vacuum action which both moves the dirt and sucks it up to control the dust. Effective for brushing large floor areas.

2 *Mops (dry)*
- Mops are used for manual dust control activity. Flat mops, floor sweepers have detachable, interchangeable mop heads for ease of maintenance and washing.
- Vee mops open up to allow the operator to mop wide corridors and large floor areas. Mop heads may be impregnated, that is, prepared, to make the dust stick to them and so be held rather than spread. Disposable mop heads are made from impregnated paper. Disposables are particularly effective where there is danger from cross-infection.
- Dry dusting mops are used for dusting high cornices, light fittings or ceilings.

3 *Mops (wet)*
- Wet mops for manual use are usually made from strands of twisted cotton. They can have detachable heads for easy maintenance. They can have long strands or short strands according to their design purpose. There are a wide range of mop buckets used with the wet mop, the bucket and press or squeezer bucket being most common. It is useful to have a double mop bucket, one side for wash liquid, the other side for clean rinse water. A wringer action is most effective.

4 *Polishers and pads*
Mechanical polishers are made in a wide range of sizes. In most cases it is necessary to spray or spread the polish on the large floor area before

Floor cleaning equipment (by courtesy of Nilfisk)

buffing up the surface with the polisher. Some polishers are able to perform all parts of the polishing operation. Interchangeable detachable pads are used for different types of floor surface and different types of finishing requirement. They are colour coded, e.g. tan, and white for buffing. The lighter the colour of the pad, the less abrasive it is.

5 *Polisher/scrubber*
Operate like the polishers but will also scrub when the correct pads are fitted, e.g. green for light and general purpose scrubbing.

6 *Vacuum suction cleaners*
Mechanical vacuum cleaners suck up and retain in a bag or cylinder all dust and waste materials. Small dry vacuums are used for dust and fine dirt.

Specialised commercial vacuums will be needed to deal with large particles of waste.

Many commercial vacuum cleaners can cope with both wet and dry suction cleaning activity. Useful in bar, storeroom, and food preparation areas.

All machines will have accessories for reaching heights or interchangeable heads to deal with particular types of waste.

7   Central vacuum systems

A suction hose is connected to a wall link. All dust is sucked to a central point for disposal.

8   Scrubbers/dryers – automatic machines

These machines have the capability of washing, rinsing and drying the

**Combined scrubber/dryer
(by courtesy of Nilfisk)**

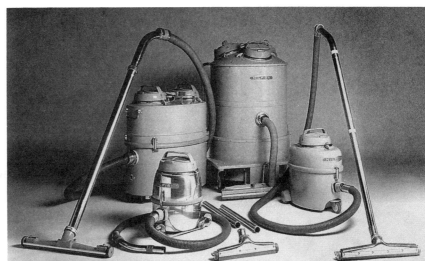

Vacuum cleaners (by courtesy of Nilfisk)

Equipment	Floors			Furniture & Fittings				Walls		Frequency		Soilage	
	–	–	–	Fabric	Plastic /glass	Metal	Wood	–	–	Daily	Weekly	Light	Heavy
	Terrazzo: Quarry Tiles	Wood Vinyl	Carpet	Curtains Upholstery	Windows Mirrors Fittings	Fittings Surfaces	Furniture	Paint Tiles Formica. Washable Wall-paper	Fabric Wall-paper				
Polishers & pads		√								√	√	√	√
Polisher/scrubber	√	√								√	√	√	√
Vacuum suction cleaners			√	√					√	√	√	√	√
Central vacuum systems wet/ dry	√	√	√							√	√	√	√
Scrubber/dryers	√	√								√	√	√	√
Shampoo spray			√								Periodic	√	√

floor in sequence as the machine passes over it. Used mainly on large floor areas.

The big machines are self propelled and the operator guides the machine direction only.

9   Shampoo – spray/extraction

Used for carpets and soft furnishing. The surface is subjected to a high pressure jet of solution to forcefully loosen the soil and dirt. This is followed by a suction action to draw the dirt and solution out of the fabric or carpet. The solution will have a solvent or detergent action. Additional brush heads can be used to provide a scrubbing action for heavily soiled surfaces.

10   Trolley

The cleaners' trolley serves to hold all cleaning agents, materials, replacements and waste sacks in a convenient form. By using a movable trolley it is possible to save both time and energy.

1   Abrasive pads

Used for moving small patches of stubborn dirt from surfaces or equipment.

Materials

2   Cloths

Fabric cloths are used for dusting and polishing. They should be soft and absorbent. For a maximum efficiency they must be washed regularly and thoroughly dried.

3   Chamois

Used for cleaning windows, mirrors, tiles and paintwork. As chamois is expensive a synthetic chamois made from non-woven fibre may be used for the same purposes.

4   Mats

Dust mats are used as a barrier to prevent dirt reaching the inside of the building. They are usually placed by doorways.

Abrasive pads (by courtesy of Vileda Ltd)

5   Paper items

For:
- (a) all cleaning purposes where disposables are required;
- (b) as part of the washing-up process;
- (c) for hand wiping. All paper items should be disposed of hygienically after use.

6   Wipes

Used for wet cleaning. Most wipes are re-usable for a limited period, particularly fabric or paper, e.g. 'J cloths'. Disposable wipes or swabs should be used where there is a danger of cross-infection. They should be hygienically disposed of in sealable sacks or by incineration.

Wipes (by courtesy of Vileda Ltd)

Cleaning schedule

This is a plan to cover all cleaning activity in a particular area.

A kitchen cleaning schedule

1 *Floor*
(a) clean spillage immediately
(b) mop with cleaning solution, rinse with clean water, mop dry.
Frequency: as required, but not less than three times per day.

2 *Work-tops*
(a) clean spillage immediately
(b) clean between each preparation process
(c) wash thoroughly using cleaning agent, rinse and wipe dry.
Frequency: as required but not less than three times per day after peak work. Special clean at least three times per week, e.g. Monday, Wednesday and Friday.

3 *Sinks*
(a) clean with freshly prepared solution
(b) rinse well with clean water.
Frequency: as required but not less than twice per day. Special clean framework and wash splash area daily.

Other items as appropriate. In each case the cleaning agent and dilution would be specified.

Cleaning standards

Cleaning standards are met by following:
1 The instructions on cleaning agents;
2 Work process cards which indicate correct method and sequence for the cleaning of a particular area
3 The cleaning schedule indicating the frequency with which each cleaning activity has to be carried out.
    The standard achieved will relate to the skill and training of the worker, the time available, the quality of the cleaning agents and materials, and the skill used to match the correct method to a particular job.

Maintenance

Maintenance of equipment and surfaces is carried out in order to:
1 Prevent unexpected breakdown of equipment and interruption of production.
2 Give a longer life to the item or the surface.
3 Save on unexpected repair cost.
4 Prevent accidents and danger to either the staff or the products.

Maintenance contracts

It is usual when a new piece of equipment or surface is installed to arrange a regular maintenance contract. This may be carried out by the supplier or an agent. The contract arrangement covers the regular periodic cleaning and maintenance of the equipment or surface, for an agreed rate of payment. In this case the maintenance will be carried out by an outside maintenance operative.
    If a company has their own maintenance staff this regular work will be carried out in the same organised way by them.

Maintenance programmes
Any maintenance programme will cover:
1 Preventative maintenance. This will be carried out on a daily basis by the staff who use the equipment or area. It covers regular and correct cleaning and checking of all fittings and correct re-assembly of items after washing or cleaning and reporting any unusual wear or damage.
2 Periodic maintenance. A fixed programme of weekly or monthly checks will be planned and carried out either by the operating staff or the company maintenance staff. This will involve special cleaning, oiling and checks on fittings (for food equipment edible oils only to be used).
3 Regular servicing. Will be carried out by specialist engineers in the case of equipment, or specialist cleaners for surfaces, e.g. extractor hoods or ceilings. Repair and replacement will be undertaken as necessary.

Maintenance records
A maintenance record card will be kept for each item of equipment or installation. It will cover detail of:
1 Item serial number, size, type, manufacturer;
2 Date of purchase, age;
3 Where it is fixed;
4 The contract servicing arrangement;
5 Date of each service carried out;
6 Date and detail of repair and replacement;
   All this information indicates how well a particular item is performing and which type of items are durable. It also shows those which are unsatisfactory or may need replacing.

Production flow/kitchen layout

Activity planning

1 Decide what type of food production system is needed, e.g.
   (a) Cook/chill or cook/freeze streamlined bulk production unit;
   (b) cook/serve bulk or call order production;
   (c) fast food, fast finish system;
   (d) salad, sandwich, snack assembly.

2 Choose equipment to suit the chosen system, e.g.
   (a) Choose the minimum amount of equipment which will serve the purpose well and make the unit versatile;
   (b) choose movable equipment where possible;
   (c) choose labour saving and fuel saving items.

3 Place the equipment to give the best production flow, e.g.
   (a) choose a flow pattern which allows the worker and the food item to flow forward from the stores area to the service area without interruption or the need to 'back-track';
   (b) plan to avoid dangerous crossed paths of activity or congestion at any one place;
   (c) leave clear, unobstructed through-routes for the movement of workers or trolleys;

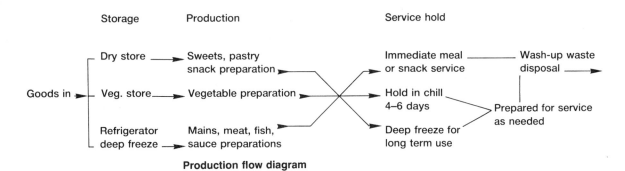

Production flow diagram

(d) position equipment to avoid danger in use and danger to passers-by;

(e) leave room around equipment for easy cleaning;

(f) plan for table space or trolley space next to each piece of fixed equipment;

(g) organise the work flow to cut out unnecessary walking;

(h) have flexible service points, sockets, gas points, and drains if possible, to allow for the movement of equipment when production needs change;

(i) place suitable lighting and ventilation systems to give safe and healthy working conditions.

Kitchen layout

Central island layout   All cooking equipment is placed in the centre of the production unit. Food handling and preparation is carried out at worktops and sinks placed around the edge of the production area. (*See* p. 80.)

Advantages:

1   Centralised cooking equipment allows for centralised services, e.g. gas, electricity and drainage.

2   It offers a pleasant outlook to workers.

3   Allows for efficient extraction of heat and steam through a central extractor hood.

4   Keeps movement of staff and materials to a minimum.

5   Offers a good general purpose production facility.

Band layout   The kitchen area is fitted with several bands. Each band is made up of cooking and preparation equipment – tables and sinks, all designed to suit the preparation of one part of the meal, e.g. one band will be used only for vegetable preparation, another for the preparation of meat dishes. (*See* p. 80.)

Advantages:

1   This layout cuts staff movement down to a minimum, cutting out danger and saving energy.

2   All specialised staff and equipment are gathered together in one area.

3   Allows for efficient extraction of heat and steam.

Central
Island layout

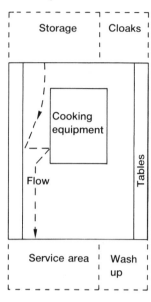

Band layout

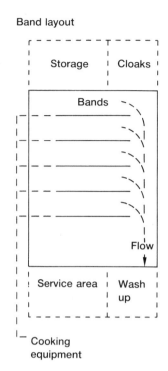

Bay layout

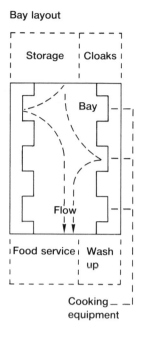

Bay layout   Each bay is set aside for a particular production purpose, e.g. one bay for preparation of meat dishes, another for sweet/pastry items. The bay contains all of the food preparation and cooking equipment for that particular type of work as well as tables, sinks and storage facilities.

Advantages:
1   All specialist staff and equipment are gathered together in one place.

Disadvantages:
1   Staff can feel cut off from what is going on in the rest of the kitchen.
2   Some equipment will be duplicated.

Back-bar layout   The equipment is usually set in a straight line behind the bar or service area. The back-bar layout serves a limited catering operation to provide a small range of food items. A limited amount of specialised equipment is included in the line up, e.g. griddle, microwave, fryer, along with a small area of preparation and service table space.

Advantages:
1   It is compact and efficient for limited cook/serve use.
2   It allows for efficient extraction of heat and steam.

Fast food/fast finish layout   A minimum amount of specialised food finishing equipment is placed immediately behind the service points. This will be made up of a range of items, including fryer, toaster, griddle, microwave. They are often controlled electronically, to give a standard quality finish and a continuous, quick flow of items.

Back bar equipment

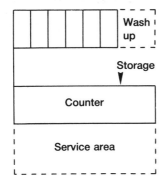

Fast food/fast finish layout

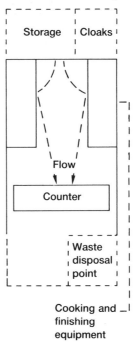

Advantages:
1   Staff movement is limited; saves time and energy and gives quick service.
2   It offers efficient extraction of heat and steam.
3   There are no crossed paths of activity.

4 THE FOOD PRODUCTION AND SERVICE PROCESS

> Menu making
> Pricing and cost control
> Production methods
> Production systems
> Service systems

Menu making

A menu is a list of the food items which are on offer to the customer in a particular eating situation. It briefly describes the item and indicates the sale price.

The menu has to be clearly displayed with correct prices for the customer to read before the meal is ordered.

The format

As menu planning is a regular and detailed activity it is useful to have a standard menu format, or empty grid or headed menu card. The format will leave space for each menu item to be clearly entered.

A set format for one day's menus

Breakfast		Mid-day		Evening	
Category	Item	Category	Item	Category	Item
Porridge		Soup		Soup	
Cold fruit		Main dish 1		Main dish 1	
Cereal		Main dish 2		Main dish 2	
Grill		Today's special		—	
Egg dish		Omelettes			
Toast		Snacks 1,2,3		Snacks 1,2,3	
Bread & butter		Veg 1,2,3		—	
Jam/marmalade		Salads 1,2,3		Salads 1,2,3	
—		Hot sweet		—	
Continental		Cold sweet		Cold sweet	
Breakfast					
				Cakes 1,2,3	

Computerised menu planning

Once the menu items have been chosen the caterer or chef will plan the production of the dishes, order the food items and work out the cost price and the selling price. It is possible to put all standard recipe information in to the computer which will prepare the food order based on standard portion size, calculate current costs, and work out the production plan as well as carrying out stock control and re-ordering.

Once the list of menu items has been decided, the rest of the planning and control activity will be performed by the computer.

Menu considerations

Customer
1 How much money does the customer wish to spend?
2 How much time is available for eating the meal?
3 What kind of appearance and presentation has most customer appeal?
4 What kind of eating area layout is most convenient and attractive?
5 Is the nutritional content and balance of the meal satisfactory?
6 Is a snack or full meal required?
7 Is it an everyday or special occasion meal?
8 Does the meal satisfy diet or ethnic or religious requirements?
9 Does the menu offer a wide variety of items? Or a fixed menu?

Production
1 What preparation space is available?
2 What preparation, cooking and finishing equipment is available?
3 Do cooking and service staff have skill to match the menu requirement?
4 Are there enough staff to cope with the menu choice?
5 How will the service of food be organised? E.g. cafeteria or waitress service, or fast food?
6 How long is the service period? How many times is each seating place to be used during this time?
7 What commodities are available fresh and for store items?
8 What is the cost of commodities?
9 How is the meal to be presented attractively: colour, texture, flavour?
10 How much profit is required?
11 What overheads, space, fuel, labour, material, have to be taken into account?
12 What type of customer is to be attracted?

Menu language

The words used to describe menu items should indicate clearly what is the main ingredient in the dish. The description should also be 'mouth watering' enough to make the customer choose a particular item. A photograph or drawing of the item helps in this process.

The menu should be written wholly in French or wholly in English. The two should never be mixed. Menu terms are a collection of words or expressions which are standard and have a generally understood meaning when used on a menu, e.g. garnish.
Some menu terms are included in the glossary.

Menu layout

A la Carte menu has:
1   A full list of all the dishes which can be prepared and served to suit customer demand – cooked to order. The diner has free choice of items.
2   Separate pricing for each item.
3   Occasional special feature items, individually priced, e.g. chef's special.
A la Carte items are part-prepared (mise-en-place) and held until the customer orders. The items will still require time for the final stages of preparation and finishing to be completed.
   The guest has to wait while the final stage of preparation is done.

Fast food menu has:
1   Some of the features of a speciality menu. It may have a basic theme item like hamburgers, fried chicken or baked potatoes.
2   Separately priced items which will be finished on demand – to order.
Fast food items are fast finish items. The basic preparation is completed up to service stage, the items are held in cool, chill, or freeze conditions until requested by a customer. At this stage they are quickly heated and served.
3   Some of the characteristics of à la Carte as it offers choice and individually-priced items.

Rotating menu cycle has:
A fixed pattern of menus to cover a fixed number of days (the menu cycle), e.g. 8 days, 15 days, 22 days. In each case the menu pattern covers a number of weeks plus one day. The menu cycle is repeated regularly but the extra day ensures that the food items as they are rotated are not repeated on fixed days of the week.

Speciality menu has:
1   A special theme or style of layout to suit one particular type of place or group of customers, e.g. vegetarian, pizza, spaghetti, chinese speciality eating houses.
2   It can be based on the à la carte pattern and offer choice *or* the table d'hôte pattern where the menu is fixed.

Special function menu has:
1   A fixed number of courses or a set collection of dishes for buffet service.
2   A fixed selling price.
When the function is booked the client will be offered several set menus to choose from. Once the menu has been selected the food will be presented to the guest as a fixed meal without opportunity for choice.

Table d'hôte menu has:
1   A fixed number of courses and fixed choice (although within each course there may be a limited choice).
2   A fixed selling price to cover the complete meal.
A table d'hôte menu may be known as a 'fixed menu' or given a special name like 'Chef's choice meal for today'.

Menu presentation

The layout and design of the menu can be used to attract the customer. Coloured card printed with the 'logo' of the eating place enhances the menu. A 'logo' will show the name of the place and a drawing to describe it.

The menu card can be large or small to suit the number of items to go on it.

The card is often inserted in a plastic holder or cover to keep it clean and pleasant for use.

The menu may be printed on paper or plastic-coated place mats or displayed in lighted strip form above the service area – as in fast food outlets.

The food service will be speeded up if the customer can see the menu well in advance and make a choice before reaching the main service area.

Portion control

In order to control portion size and value and give cost control and customer satisfaction, *do*

1 Match portion size to what the customer needs, e.g. age, activity and time available for eating the food.

2 Match the portion size to what the customer can afford and accept as a competitive price for the item.

3 Provide standard portions of identical quality and size.

4 Use standard portion containers or individual portion containers in the food production area.

5 Base standard portion size on standard recipes, methods, and quality and yield controlled ingredients.

Portion indicator

Item	Portion allowance per person		Portion yield (approx) per	
	Metric	*Imperial*	*Litre/kg*	*Pint/lb*
Soup	200 ml	6 fl oz	5 per litre	3 per pt
Sauce	75 ml	2 fl oz	14 per litre	10 per pt
Meat	—	—	—	—
off the bone	100–125 g	4–5 oz	8 per kg	4 per lb
on the bone	150–175 g	6–7 oz	6 per kg	2–3 per lb
Fish	100–125 g	4–5 oz	8 per kg	4 per lb
Potatoes	—	—	—	—
boiled	100–125 g	4–5 oz	8 per kg	4 per lb
fried chips	150–200 g	6–8 oz	6 per kg	2–3 per lb
2nd vegetable	100–125 g	4–5 oz	8 per kg	4 per lb
Pastry	25 g	1 oz	34 per kg	16 per lb
Sponge	25 g	1 oz	34 per kg	16 per lb
Hot/cold drinks	200 ml	6 fl oz	5 per litre	3 per pt

6   Use pre-prepared, pre-weighed and pre-packed products where suitable.

7   Avoid waste of portions through over-preparation, over-cooking and over-portioning.

8   Use portion control serving aids at the point of service.

9   Train staff to know portion sizes and to use standard portioning equipment and procedures.

10   Check all food waste left by the customer and adjust portion size and quality in relation to the quantity and type of food which the customer leaves on the plate.

Pricing and cost control

Careful pricing calculations and cost control practices have to be applied to the running of any business where the making of profit and the avoidance of loss is involved.

Cost control runs through all the stages of the purchasing, production and service process.

Cost control

This covers:
1   Ordering, buying, issuing control;
2   Production and quality control;
3   Waste and loss control;
4   The accurate calculation of cost and profit.

Computerised cash control

Computerised cash control tills are usually situated on the service counter or in the main service area. They are not just convenient and secure cash boxes, but are very sophisticated machines. For the food service operator they are easy to use.

The cash control tills are able to:
1   'Check in' the food service assistant at the start and 'check out' at the end of the work period.
2   Record the menu items required by the individual customer, as the dishes are ordered.
3   Show a breakdown of the number and type of items sold during a particular part of the service period, e.g. peak hour volume.
4   Total the sale price of meal and print a receipt. The till keys may show cash amounts or be labelled with menu item names or the item code number. As the chosen key is pressed, the appropriate amount is recorded. It will also show how much change is to be given to the customer.
5   Flash order information to a display screen in the kitchen or servery area.
6   Record the stock items as they are used and keep an up-to-date stock record.
Note: Items 5 and 6 will only be possible on more expensive computer till systems.

A computer cash control system is very compact and quick to operate. It avoids the use of large quantities of paper for accounting and stock records. It collects together in one place a lot of cash, demand and general business information and cuts down the possibility of error in cash handling and order taking. Loss of cash and goods through pilfering is reduced when computerised cash control systems are used. They are also a time-saving aid.

Cash flow

Any business operation has a flow of cash coming into it from sales to customers and a flow of money leaving it to pay for wages, fuel, maintenance, commodities, replacement and development.

Incoming cash → Cash flow → Outgoing cash

In order to keep the business running there must be always enough money coming in to pay the bills. If not, borrowing will be necessary. The interest paid on borrowed money will add to the general costs and reduce profit. This shortage of cash occurs when:
1 Goods and services are not being sold fast enough;
2 Goods and services are not being sold in enough volume or quantity;
3 Customers fail to pay their bills fast enough. Shortage of in-coming cash leads to cost-cutting, lowering of standards and eventually to close down.

Food sales

Costs The cost involved in meal production can be broken down into:
1 Food costs
2 Labour cost, e.g. wages
3 Overhead cost, e.g. fuel, lighting, maintenance.
These costs form the basis for the calculation of the selling price.

Gross profit/kitchen profit Calculated by deducting the cost of food only from the selling price.

Gross profit = selling price − food cost

This forms the basis for calculating net profit.

Net profit The amount that remains after labour and overheads have been deducted from the gross profit.

$$\text{Gross profit} - \text{labour cost} - \text{overheads} = \text{net profit}$$

Selling price The selling price of an item can be calculated to a formula:

$$\text{Selling price} = \frac{\text{cost of food materials} \times 100}{\text{food cost (\%)}}$$

A typical breakdown for a catering operation might be, for example,

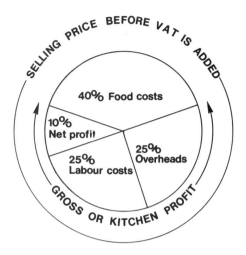

40% food cost + 25% labour cost + 25% overheads + 10% net profit = 100% selling price before VAT
+ VAT = selling price inclusive of VAT

Variation in profit 1 To encourage a high level of sales and a good turnover of customers it is usual to keep the profit rate down to a level which matches the competition of other catering outlets nearby.
2 The profit rate has to give the owner a fair return for his work effort and cash investment.
3 High rates of profit can only be achieved where the quality of the product or service is exceptionally good or where the customer is willing to pay for scarce products, space and privacy.

VAT All food, drink and accommodation charges quoted to the customer must by law be inclusive of VAT. The amount printed in the list of charges will be the final amount the customer is expected to pay. The % rate of VAT is fixed by the government and is at present 15%.

Production methods

Conversion tables

Cooking and storage temperature guide

F	C
475	240 Very hot oven
450	230 Hot oven
375	190 Deep frying maximum
350	180 Deep frying general
325	160 Moderate oven
275	140 Cool oven
250	130 Very cool oven
212	100 Boiling water
180	82 Dishwashing rinse water

(contd.)

Cooking and storage temperature guide *(contd.)*

F	C	
160	71	Hot cupboard food storage
145	62	Maximum dishwashing water
140	60	
		Between these temperatures there is the greatest danger of bacterial growth and development in food
42	6	Refrigeration for vegetables
40	5	Refrigeration for dairy products
38	3	
34	1	General purpose refrigeration
32	0	
0	−18	
−20	−29	Frozen food storage

Cooking temperatures

Centigrade (C)	Fahrenheit (F)	Gas mark	Temperature
130	250	½	
140	275	1	Cool
150	300	2	
160	325	3	Warm
180	350	4	Moderate
190	375	5	
200	400	6	
220	425	7	Hot
230	450	8	
240	475	9	Very Hot

Length

1 metre (m) = 100 centimetres (cm) = 1000 millimetres (mm) = 39 ins.

3 mm = $\frac{1}{8}$ in
5 mm = $\frac{1}{4}$ in
10 mm (1 cm) = $\frac{1}{2}$ in
2 cm = $\frac{3}{4}$ in
2.5 cm = 1 in
4 cm = $1\frac{1}{2}$ in
5 cm = 2 in
10 cm = 4 in

Liquid capacity

1 litre (l) = 1000 millilitres (ml) = $1\frac{3}{8}$ pints (35 fluid ozs)

25 ml = 1 fluid oz
50 ml = 2 fluid oz
100 ml = 4 fluid oz
150 ml = 5 fluid oz
600 ml = 20 fluid oz = 1 pint

Weight

1 kilogram (kg) = 1000 grams (g) = approximately 2 lb 4 oz.

25 grams	= 1 oz approx
50 g	= 2 oz approx
100–125 g	= 4 oz approx
225 g	= 8 oz approx
325–350 g	= 12 oz approx
450 g	= 16 oz approx
½ kg = 500 g	= 17½ oz approx
1 kg	= 2 lb 4 oz approx

The cooking process

Foods are cooked in order to:
1   Make them easy to eat and digest.
2   Vary their texture, flavour and appearance and make them more attractive.
3   Destroy harmful bacteria.

Conducted heat
Is the movement of heat directly from one solid item to another through contact. The heat travels through the solid material e.g. metals.

Convected heat
In convection heat passes through a liquid or gas. It relies on the movement of gas or liquid which rises when heated, e.g. hot air moving round an oven or boiling water moving round a pan. In forced air oven convection a fan assists this natural movement.

Infra red
Infra red heat waves travel in straight lines heating only the food which is touched by the waves and not the atmosphere through which the waves pass.
Infra red rays produce a gentle, steady and uniform heat. It is an efficient heat source.

Microwaves
The magnetron in the microwave oven generates microwaves (high frequency radio waves). These cause the molecules in the food to jostle together and transfer heat through the food by friction. There is no browning effect.

Radiant heat
Radiant heat travels in straight rays direct from the heat source to the food, e.g. grilling or spit roasting on an open fire or over gas jets.

Induction cooking
Is a new development. It is used for top stove work – cooking vegetables, soups, sauces.
   The flat hob is made of vitrioceramic material, with up to 6 cooking plates. The plates have ten control positions ranging from low simmer to boil.

Induction cooking occurs when a magnetic field is brought into contact with an iron based pan. The pan then becomes its own cooking element and is responsible for the rapid heating which takes place inside it.

The magnetic field is made by a generator under the cooking plates. Only iron-based pans can be used.

Induction cooking is very economical as the current is used *only* for the length of time that the pan is in contact with the plate.

It is a quick, safe and clean form of cooking. The plate itself does not feel hot to the touch, reducing the risk of burns, and the area around the induction cooker is cool to work in.

Methods of cooking

Baking Baked foods are cooked in dry oven conditions where the heat source is radiant or convected.

Steam is involved in the process as it is naturally released from food during cooking.

Use:
For
1   Meat and fish
2   Pastry and sweet items
3   Vegetables and potatoes.
For specialised bakery use, steam injection may be used to give the required degree of moisture.

Equipment:
1   Gas, electric, or solid fuel oven ranges.
2   Forced air convection oven.
3   Convection/steam injection ovens.
4   Single or tiered shallow baking ovens.

Boiling Boiled foods are completely covered by a liquid – stock or water – during the cooking process.

The heat is conducted to the water by direct contact between the pan and the boiling ring.

Within the pan, convection ensures the movement of heat through the boiling water and around the meat or vegetables item being cooked.

Once boiling point has been reached, most of the cooking process will be carried out at controlled simmer.

Use:
1   Meat & poultry
2   Vegetables
3   Stock

Equipment:
1   For small quantities – saucepans.
2   For large quantities – boiling pans.
3   Bratt pans.

Braising   Braising is a combination of stewing and roasting. The meat or vegetables are sealed by quick frying and then placed on a bed of vegetables with a small amount of liquid. A tight lid is used.

Part way through the cooking process, the lid is removed and the meat or vegetables are allowed to brown.

This method reduces shrinkage, develops the flavour and retains the nutritive value of the food. The liquid should be served as part of the dish, or as a base for gravy.

Use:
1   Medium cuts of meat.
2   Poultry.
3   Vegetables.

Equipment:
1   For small quantities – casserole.
2   For large quantities – oven tins and lids.

Frying deep/shallow   Frying is a quick method of cooking. It is achieved by placing the food item in pre-heated deep or shallow fat or oil.

The temperature or type of fat or oil must be carefully controlled to match the requirement for each particular food item being cooked.

Deep fat frying temperature/time guide

Temperature	Item	Time
190°C or 375°F	chips from raw to serve chips to brown after blanching	4–6 mins 1½–2 mins
180°C or 350°F	coated fish fritters made up meat items yeast items	3–5 mins 3–5 mins 4–6 mins 4–6 mins
160°C or 325°F	coated meat or poultry	8–12 mins
150°C or 300°F	potatoes/chips for blanching	2–4 mins

Use:
Deep frying
1   Coated meat and fish.
2   Fritters.
3   Made up meat items, e.g. croquettes.
4   Vegetables, e.g. chips.
5   Yeast goods.
Shallow frying
1   Fish.
2   Good cuts of meat.
3   Pancakes.
4   Pre-sealing and browning off (for braising, sauté and stewing)

Equipment:
Deep frying
1   Deep fat fryer, timer or computer-controlled
2   Friture
Shallow frying
1   Bratt pan (large quantity)
2   Crêpe pan.
3   Frying pan, large or small.
4   Sauté pan.

Griddle/fry plate   The griddle or fry plate is a solid metal plate. Food is placed directly on its pre-heated, lightly greased surface for quick cooking.

Thicker meat items should be turned over during cooking to brown both surfaces and ensure that the food is cooked right through.

Use:
For quick/demand cooking of individual portion items, e.g.
1   Eggs.
2   Hamburgers.
3   Meat, e.g. steaks.

Equipment:
Griddle/fry plate.

Grilling   Grilling is carried out using direct or radiant heat.

Grilling under heat For grilling under heat the food is placed on the grill rack and held under the pre-heated grill burner until the food is brown and thoroughly cooked.

Meat and fish should be brushed with fat at regular intervals to prevent shrinkage.

Use:
For foods which can be cooked quickly.
1   Fish.
2   Good cuts of meat, e.g. steaks.
3   Poultry.
4   Any item which needs to be browned, e.g. cheese, breadcrumbs or sauce-topped items.

Equipment:
For grilling under heat radiant grills and infra red grills are used.

Grilling over heat For grilling over heat the food is placed on a preheated, pregreased grilling rack and left to become brown and thoroughly cooked.

The appearance of the item and thoroughness of the cooking will be assisted by turning the item over at regular intervals.

Use:
1   Fish.
2   Good cuts of meat.
3   Poultry.

Equipment:
Chargrill and charbroiler.

Microwave In microwave ovens food is cooked as a result of the activity of high frequency radio waves, generated by the magnetron. Food is cooked evenly all through, the centre cooking at the same time and rate as the outside. This is different from the other methods where heat moves from the outside of the item and gradually penetrates to the centre.

The microwave oven itself remains cool while cooking is in progress. So do the containers in which the food is held. Porcelain, paper or specially manufactured containers must be used.

No item made of metal or with a metal decoration or rim can be used as this causes the microwaves to be reflected back into the magnetron and causes serious damage to the microwave oven.

It is important to place the food carefully on the plate to give an even distribution and density, when cooking or reheating food items. This allows all of the food items to reach the same temperature in the same period of time. If this is not done some food will be hot while other items stay cool.

Microwave cooking does not brown the food. It is therefore necessary to:
1 Brown food items before they are put into the microwave, e.g. quick fry first.
2 Brown food after it comes out of the microwave, e.g. grill.
3 Use a combined microwave/browner which performs both functions.

Use:
1 Cooking raw foods.
2 Defrosting frozen foods.
3 Reheating completely prepared foods to give a fast finish.
4 Coping quickly with a small, steady and often irregular customer demand.
5 Where it is necessary to heat or cook large numbers of items quickly at one time a microwave/convection oven can be used. This gives some of the speed advantage of the microwave oven, combined with the larger capacity and efficiency of the forced air convection oven.

Equipment:
Microwave oven, microwave/browning oven, microwave/convection oven, microaire oven.

Poaching Poached foods are cooked slowly in seasoned liquid, e.g. water or milk, in a shallow pan. The liquid should be kept near to boiling point, but never actually boil. This is a gentle method of cooking which preserves the texture of food and makes it easy to digest. It also helps to retain the flavour.

This is an ideal cooking method to use when feeding young children, invalids or those with digestive problems.

Use:
1   Eggs.
2   Fish.
3   Fruit.
4   Poultry.

Equipment:
For small quantities:
1   Frying pan;
2   Shallow-sided pan.
For large quantities:
A bratt pan.

Roasting (oven roasting and spit roasting)   Roasting is achieved by applying direct or radiant heat to the food and adding fat.

The direct heat seals the surface and develops the colour and flavour of the food.

Traditionally, the term 'roast' is used for meat and vegetables cooked on a spit or rotating rod over an open fire, or the gas jets of a modern roto-spit.

Today the term is also applied to oven cooked meats which have been left uncovered during cooking and basted regularly with fat.

Use:
1   Better joints of meat.
2   Made up meat items.
3   Poultry.
4   Vegetables, e.g. potatoes.

Equipment:
1   Gas, electric or solid fuel oven ranges.
2   Forced air convection oven.
3   Roasting oven.
4   Slow roasting oven.
5   Roto spit (barbecue oven).
6   Open fire (outdoor).

Steaming   Steaming is a method of cooking food in moist heat. This softens the food and cooks it without browning.

Steamed foods are easy to digest and are therefore suitable for children, invalids and those with digestive problems.

Steamed items can be finished by other methods in order to brown the food, e.g. by grilling, roasting or deep fat frying.

Pressure steamers speed up the steaming process. They are efficient for batch cooking use.

Pressureless convection steamers speed up the process even more, to such an extent that they can be used as part of the fast-finish food operation.

Pressureless steamers retain the colour, texture, flavour and nutrients in the food.

Use:
1 Fish.
2 Meat.
3 Poultry.
4 Puddings.
5 Vegetables.
6 Prepared frozen food items, particularly vegetables (pressure steamers).
7 Defrosting and heating of frozen foods in batches for immediate/demand service, as part of cook/freeze or fast finish food service operation (pressureless steamers).

Equipment:
1 Atmospheric steamers – small or large.
2 Roto-pan steamer.
3 Pressure steamer, small or large.
4 Pressureless convection steamer, small or large.

Stewing Stewed items are cooked slowly in a small amount of liquid, e.g. stock for savoury items, syrup for sweet items. The long slow cooking helps to tenderise the meat, develop the flavour and reduce shrinkage.

   The nutrients from the food flow into the cooking liquor, which is usually made into a sauce and is served as part of the dish.

   Prepared meat for stews is usually fried quickly to help develop the colour and flavour before the cooking liquor is added.

   Food can be stewed in pans over burners or in the oven.

Use:
1 Medium cuts of meat.
2 Fruit.
3 Poultry.

Equipment:
Small quantities:
1 Stew pan with lid.
2 Sauté pan with lid.
3 Casserole-oven method.
For large quantities:
1 Boiling pan.
2 Bratt pan.
3 Oven tin with lid (oven method).

Food production systems

Conventional cook/ serve A cook/serve system is any system where the food is served immediately after production. It may be served directly from the production unit over a service counter or centrally plated (e.g. Ganymede) or served in bulk containers in the production unit, ready for direct transport to the satellite feeding units or other service point.

   Traditional cooking methods will be used for the systematically organised bulk or batch production.

For direct restaurant service traditional mise-en-place (part pre-preparation finishing methods) may be used.

Use:
1 Hospitals – for counter, trolley or Ganymede service.
2 Schools, colleges, universities for cafeteria, family or waitress service.
3 Industry for staff and works restaurants.
4 Hotels and restaurants for waiter, buffet or cafeteria service.

Cook/chill   Cook/chill systems are designed to allow complete preparation of food items to be carried out under streamlined, controlled production circumstances. Chill foods are prepared and brought down to their 'holding' chill temperature of +3°C by being passed through a blast chiller. To make sure that the appearance, flavour, nutritional value and texture of the food is kept, it is importance to reduce the temperature rapidly. Food packed not more than 2" (50 mm) in depth should take no longer than 90 minutes to chill to +3°C (38°F).

Chilled foods must be held in a refrigerator at +3°C and used only for this purpose, until they are required for vending or finishing. They can be kept, at most, for 5 days.

The central production allows for quality and portion control, buying advantage for commodities and the reduced cost of bulk production. It allows food to be produced in one place and eaten in another and so cuts out the need for a fully or partly equipped production kitchen near to the point of service. The system flow is:

cook → chill → store (hold) → distribute → regenerate → serve.

Chilled foods must be transported in temperature controlled carrying boxes to avoid any rise in temperature during a journey.

As chill foods remain above freezing point at all stages of production and storage, there is *no* need for special ingredients and recipes. Usual tested recipes can be used.

Chill items take less time and less fuel to finish than do frozen foods as the storage, holding temperature is higher.

Chill foods can be finished using normal cooking equipment or fast finish equipment, e.g. microwave, convection oven, infra-red, fryer, or pressureless steamer.

Use:
This is a most versatile system. It is usually associated with bulk production but it can be used on a small scale where staff time or space are scarce, e.g. pub catering.

Bulk chilling and refrigeration is used for:
1 Hotels and conference centres for banqueting.
2 Hospitals.
3 Schools.
4 Universities and residential establishments.
5 Large office blocks.
6 Meals on wheels.

Regethermic   This is a complete planned system for cook chill which uses equipment designed for the purpose.

Chill items can be stored in individual or bulk portion packs. It is based on centralised food production using normal equipment.

Where large batches of food are produced rege-stacker trolleys may be used to carry prepared foods directly in to the oven without the need to unload or transfer goods. From the oven they are wheeled into the blast chiller and then directly into the walk-in chill 'hold' storage space.

This system offers a complete separation of the food production and food service operations.

Regeneration (re-heating) is done at the point of eating, e.g. the ward or the individual dining room, using portable Regethermic thermal regeneration units.

Cook/freeze   Cook/freeze systems are designed to allow complete preparation of food items to be carried out under controlled production circumstances. The complete foods are brought *quickly* to an acceptable deep freeze holding temperature of between 0°F to −20°F (−18°C to −29°C), i.e. below freezing point, by being passed through a blast-freeze unit.

Deep frozen items can be stored in the correct deep freeze storage conditions for long periods of time until needed for use.

This system allows the production activity and the service activity to be separated and for food items to be centrally produced by the catering unit itself or by a manufacturer. This leads to uniform products, quality and portion control, buying advantage for commodities and reduced costs due to bulk production. Items can be individually portioned or bulk packaged before freezing.

As freezing can affect the flavour, texture and appearance of some food items, special recipes have to be followed and in some cases special ingredients have to be used, e.g. modified starch for sauce making.

Incorrect thawing can lead to the development of harmful bacteria. All deep frozen items must be thawed slowly and thoroughly (e.g. in normal refrigeration) or very quickly (e.g. in microwave) according to the instructions for each particular item.

Note: No deep frozen item should be re-deep frozen once it has been thawed for use.

Prepared deep frozen items must be transported in refrigerated vans.

Frozen items can be finished (made ready for eating) using normal cooking equipment. Frozen items can be added to conventionally cooked dishes or heated in microwaves, convection or infra-red units, or fryers.

Use:

1   For any catering outlet where a wide range of items are offered, but staff and equipment are kept to a minimum.

The emphasis moves from basic production to good quality finishing and presentation.

2   Any catering operation which has several satellite eating areas, e.g. large hospitals with dining rooms spread about the site, large industrial

sites or 'meals on wheels' where individual frozen meals are delivered to diners in their own homes.

Fast finish Fast finish foods rely on a mixture of the three main production/service systems. Fast finish foods offer a hot or cold meal item on customer demand.

Any fast finish food system is made up of three elements:

1 Food items which are pre-prepared to the point of being complete and ready to serve.

These can be conventionally produced or bought ready prepared or batch produced for chilling, or mass produced or purchased for freezing.

2 A storage or 'hold' situation.

This can be cool-store or vending machine, controlled chill storage or vending facility, deep freeze store or vending facility.

3 A fast finish re-heating facility.

This can be direct customer vend/service, customer vend/microwave/service.

Alternatively fast food operatives heat food in microwave, convection, grill, fryer or infra-red unit.

Use:

In any catering outlet where fast service is required, e.g. High Street quick food outlets, rail or bus stations, exhibitions, large sporting events.

Food service systems

Back-bar As back-bar food items are cooked to order and served over the normal bar counter, the cooking and serving has to be a quick and simple operation. The food will be eaten at bar tables and it is important that the clearing of waste and dirty dishes is done regularly and efficiently. Food may be served in baskets, on plates or in metal or disposable containers.

Use:

1 Licensed house catering.
2 Bars.
3 Clubs.
4 Small party rooms.

Banqueting The layout of tables for a banqueting function is usually agreed with the client after suggestions have been put forward to them by the banqueting manager. Particular attention will be paid to the seating of key guests and speakers. For very formal occasions a top table with sprigs will be used. For less formal functions a large number of small tables seating 8–12 people will be assembled to a pre-agreed plan. An agreed set menu is used.

Use:

1 Special functions.
2 Company or club dinners.

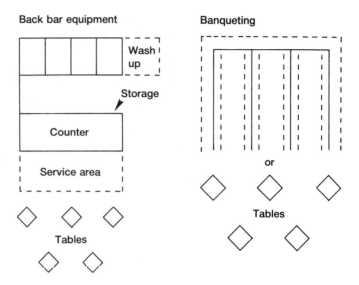

3 Weddings.
4 Conferences.

Buffet/self-service

Buffet-self or waiter service

Buffet service is used mainly for cold items, but with the addition of hot plates or fixed, heated buffet bars it is possible to serve hot food. A selection of pre-portioned items are displayed. The diner makes his own choice and generally serves himself. Diners either stand up to eat or take the food back to fully-prepared or side-tables. A more expensive buffet service operation may use chefs or service staff to carve meat, portion sweets and generally assist the diner by carrying out the more skilled portioning and service tasks.

Use:
1 Restaurants and function operations.
2 Weddings.
3 Conferences.
4 Meetings.
5 Lunch clubs.

Counter service

1 Cafeteria
This is the most versatile and widely used form of service.
It is a diner self-service system:
the diner collects a tray and walks along the service counter choosing food items. The flow of diners is controlled by a barrier to avoid people leaving the system without paying for food. Food items are laid out in order:
(*a*) menu display and trays;
(*b*) cold sweets, cold drinks, salads;
(*c*) main items and vegetables;
(*d*) hot sweets, hot drinks;
(*e*) cash till, cutlery;
(*f*) tray racks or conveyor for clearing.

Cafeteria service

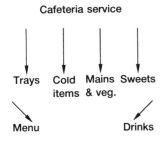

The customer carries the meal to a free table. Clearing is done either by the diner or by clearing staff, who dispose of waste food and dirty crockery onto racks or a conveyor clearing belt.

Use:

Large or small scale operations, i.e. schools, colleges and universities; transport and industrial. Used anywhere where a *choice* of meal items is offered and a quick informal system is needed. It uses the minimum of service and clearing staff.

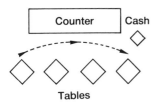

2   Fast finish food – take-away

The counter is the key to this type of service operation. The system is designed to give speedy and efficient service to a regular stream of people. All of the items ordered by a customer are collected up by the service operative and served from a single point. The fast food service counter can be approached directly by the customer who selects the service/cash point with least people waiting. This gives a calm but fast form of service and avoids queueing.

Use:

Fast food operations, i.e. hamburger, chicken, pizza, fish & chips, and take-away.

3   Free flow

Free flow is another form of counter service. It offers some of the speed and efficiency of a fast-food service counter by allowing the customer to approach directly a particular part of the service counter set aside for one type of food item, e.g. salads. If the diner requires only one type of food item it is fast, but it can be a slow form of service for the diner who wishes to collect up items from several sections of the counter. It may involve joining a queue at each one before the complete meal is collected.

Use:

As for cafeteria.

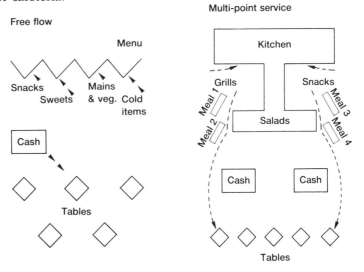

4   *Multi-point*
A type of counter service, the organisation of multi-point is more elaborate. Separate areas are set aside for particular types of food items or complete meals, e.g. salad bar, grill-bar, set meal 1, set meal 2, snacks. It is more efficient than free flow for the diner who wishes to choose a set meal.

Use:
As for cafeteria but used mainly in very large dining areas, e.g. hospitals, industry and large office blocks.

Plate service 1   This is a form of table/waiter service. It is used with table d'hôte or a fixed menu. The complete meal is plated in the kitchen or servery area and then carried quickly by the service staff to the table. For very large dining rooms, plate carriers, holding 6–8 plates may be used. This is a very quick and efficient method to use with large numbers of diners and where the service time is limited. A conveyor belt system can be used to help speed up the plating part of the operation.

Use:
1   Banquets.   4   Holiday centres.
2   Party meals.   5   Residential homes and schools.
3   Conference centres.

Central plate 2   As with plate service a complete meal is assembled before being pre-
(Ganymede)   sented to the diner. With central plate the meals are served in the kitchen area and then transported to wards or dining rooms some distance away from the production unit. The meals are individually plated to suit the patient or diner's needs. Meal order forms are completed for each person the day before the meal is required. The kitchen prepares bulk food to meet the total amount required. A conveyor belt with bain marie and service staff on either side is used to speed up the plating process. Each diner has a tray with the pre-order card on it. Each service plate has its own pre-heated base and lid which keeps the food in good condition for 1–2 hours; completed trays are slotted into unheated trolleys ready for transport to wards or dining rooms. After the meal, all plate waste, dirty plates and crockery are returned to a central wash-up area.

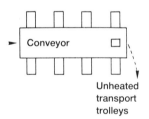

Unheated
transport
trolleys

Use:
Hospitals or any large feeding situation with satellite service points, e.g. factory and large office blocks.

Silver service   Silver service is based on a high level of personal attention for the customer: a high staff/customer ratio. It requires waiting staff with specialised skills and the correct specialised serving equipment. It is used for more elaborate meals where the customer has time to enjoy the intricacy of the service and is prepared to pay more for the added staff attention. Each food item will be presented to the customer in its complete, decorated form, before being portioned at a side table and then served. All food items are served by the waiting staff under the direction of the station waiter and head waiter. Meat may be carved at the table from a serving trolley and sweet trolleys, hors d'oeuvre trolleys will be used to display food. Food may be cooked at the table, using a gueridon trolley. A wine waiter will advise and serve the wine.

Use:
Small or large restaurants where the customers are prepared to pay for the high level of skill and the time involved in the more elaborate form of food service. The food service is regarded as an 'interest point' in the enjoyment of the total meal experience.

Half/silver
In half/silver service the meat item is already plated but other items are served. This provides a quicker and cheaper form of waitress/waiter service.

Vending Is a form of service which is carried out using automatic machines. It requires a maintenance/loading/cash control operative to look after several machines.
Vending allows customers to purchase drinks, snacks, meal items at any time of day or night.
It can be used to supplement an ordinary feeding situation, e.g. a drinks dispenser in a busy hotel, coffee shop or hospital staff dining room. It can also be used as part of a chill/vend/microwave automatic full meal, self service system.

Use:
In any situation where food, drinks, snacks are required, outside the normal dining-room situation e.g.
1 corridors in office blocks,   3 rail or bus stations.
2 factory work shops,

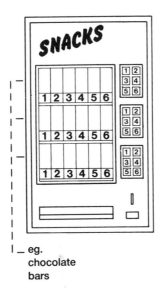

eg.
chocolate
bars

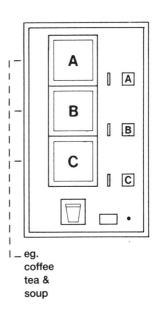

eg.
coffee
tea &
soup

5 RAW MATERIALS FOR CATERING

> Commodities
> Food science aspects
> Nutrition
> Stores and stock control

Commodities

Dairy goods

Cheese Cheese should be purchased carefully and judged by its fresh appearance. It should be avoided if it has 'sweated' or carries an 'off' smell.

Correct storage is essential to maintain the quality and flavour of cheese. If the temperature is too high the cheese will sweat, if it is too low flavour will be lost.

All cheese should be carefully wrapped or covered and kept in a cool dark area at 5°C or 40°F.

Storage in the refrigerator for long periods will affect both the texture and the flavour of cheese.

Item	Country of Origin	Cream	Blue vein	Hard	Soft
Bel Paese	Italy			X	
Brie	France				X
Boursin	France	X			
Camembert	France				X
Carré de l'est	France				X
Caerphilly	England			X	
Cheddar	England			X	
Cheshire	England			X	
Demi-Sel	France	X			
Derby	England			X	
Danish Blue	Denmark		X		
Edam	Holland			Firm	
Emmental	Switzerland			X	
Gouda	Holland			Firm	
Gorgonzola	Italy		X		
Gruyère	Switzerland			X	
Lancashire	England			X	
Leicestershire	England			X	
Parmesan	Italy			X	
Stilton	England		X		
St Paulin	France			Firm	
Wensleydale	England		X		
White Stilton	England			X	
White Wensleydale	England			X	

Cream   *Clotted cream*
A very firm, pale yellow spreading cream with a high fat content of 54%.

Use:
With jam for afternoon tea items, e.g. scones, and fruit bread.

Double cream
A thick flowing cream with a high fat content – usually 48%. It is homogenised and can be served without whisking or may be very lightly whipped.

Use:
As a decoration for sweet dishes and cakes or as a separate accompaniment. It is also used as an ingredient in cold sweets, e.g. bavarois.

Single cream
Has a lower fat content – usually 18% – and is generally homogenised. It has a pouring consistency and is not suitable for whipping. It can be UHT treated for long-life.

Use:
Added to soup and sauces or used as a pouring cream to accompany sweet dishes. Served with coffee.

Whipping cream
This cream whips easily. It has a fat content of 35% and can be used un-whipped if required. It is never homogenised.

Use:
Whipped and added to fruit or cold custard dishes. Used to decorate cakes and sweets or served as an accompaniment.

Eggs   *Egg-dried*
The fresh egg is processed by film or spray drying. This removes the moisture content and gives a long storage life to the product.

Use:
Suitable for all cooking purposes. Dried whole egg is easily contaminated once water has been added and should be used quickly.

Egg-fresh
The white of the egg is largely protein and water. The yolk is protein, fat and fat soluble vitamins and water. The shell is largely calcium. Eggs are graded for size and weight in line with EEC regulations, in 5 g steps.
Grade 1: 70 g+
       2: 65–70 g
       3: 60–65 g
       4: 55–60 g
       5: 50–55 g
       6: 45–50 g
       7: 45 g or less

Use:
For baking and main dishes. Eggs are used for the qualities of:
1   adding food value
2   binding
3   coating
4   glazing
5   raising – by trapping air
6   setting
7   thickening.
Fresh eggs should be stored in dark, cool conditions.

Eggs-liquid
The shells are commercially removed to give liquid whole egg. The yolks and the whites can be bought separately. It is quick to use, easy to measure and quality controlled.

Use:
For large quantity or commercial baking. Liquid egg must be stored under normal refrigeration.

Eggs-frozen
The yolks and the whites are frozen separately.

Use:
Frozen egg must be kept frozen in deep freeze until required for use. Must be used immediately after thawing.

Milk *Condensed milk*
The milk is preserved by removing water and adding sugar. The whole or skimmed milk is homogenised and heated to 176°F or 80°C for 15 minutes. Sugar is added, the water evaporated under a vacuum and the milk canned and sealed.

Use:
For cold sweets and confectionery, and diluted for addition to drinks.

Storage life:
Long-life

Dried milk
The whole milk is homogenised and spray-dried. The milk may be skimmed before drying to reduce the fat content.

Use:
General cooking use, and for addition to drinks.

Storage life:
Long-life in powder form. Use immediately once water has been added.

Evaporated milk
Twice as concentrated as fresh milk, as water has been evaporated off. The cans are heat sterilised for 20 minutes at 240°F (115°C).

Use:
As an accompaniment to cold sweets – diluted and added to drinks.

Storage life:
Long-life.

Liquid milk
Cow's milk is made up of 88% water, approximately 4% protein, 4% butter fat, 4% carbohydrate and minerals, e.g. calcium and vitamins.

1 Homogenised
The milk has been pasteurised and processed to break up the fat globules. The fat particles are then suspended evenly through the mixture. There is no cream on top.

Use:
Sweet and savoury cooking, e.g. sauce, batter, milk puddings, and added to hot and cold drinks.

Storage life:
1–2 days in a cool place.

2   Pasteurised
Cow's milk is heated to 161°F (71°C) for 15 seconds and then it is rapidly cooled to not more than 50°F (10°C). There is very little loss of nutritional value. All harmful organisms are removed.

Storage life:
1–2 days in a cool place. 3–4 days in a refrigerator.

3   Sterilised
The milk is pre-heated, homogenised, bottled and sealed. The sealed bottles are then heated to 220°F (104°C) for 20–30 minutes and then allowed to cool.

Storage life:
One week in cool conditions, two weeks in a refrigerator. Use immediately once opened.

4   UHT (Ultra Heat Treated)
The milk is heated under pressure to 270°F or (132°C) for one second. It is also homogenised.

Storage life:
Long-life; several months unopened. Use immediately once opened.

Dry goods

Beverages   *Drinking chocolate*
A mix of cocoa powder, dried milk, and a sweetening agent, usually sugar.

Use:
mainly used as a hot drink. Can be added to cakes and sweet items.

Cocoa
Processed from the cocoa bean to give a smooth fatty liquid. Some of the fat is removed and the liquid is processed further to give a fine, dry, darkish brown powder.

Use: as a hot drink. It can be added to cakes and sweets to give colour and flavour.

Coffee
The beans are dried and eventually roasted to develop flavour to the level required for a particular strength of coffee.

Use:
coffee can be
1   whole, ground and percolated for use;
2   pre-packed, ground and percolated for use;
3   pre-prepared in instant powder form and made-up by adding boiling water.

Generally served with milk or cream. Spirits can be added for special use.

Tea

Tea is produced from dried leaves. There is a wide range of flavours depending on the type of leaf, grade, and the particular blend. Indian tea is most commonly used as a beverage.

Use:
1   China tea – not generally used, served on its own or with lemon.
2   herb teas – a delicate, specialised taste, served on their own.
3   Indian tea, served with milk or lemon.

Cereals – General

Arrowroot

This fine white powder is made from the dried milled root of the Maranta plant.

Use:

for thickening sauces and for glaze. It gives a transparent quality to sauces.

Cornflour

Is produced from the maize grain. It is 100% starch.

Use:

for thickening sauces and for glaze. Cornflour gives a slight cloudiness to a sauce.

Oats

Can be fine, medium, or coarse. They are rolled for use and are partly-cooked during the process.

Use:

for cakes and biscuits, porridge and breakfast cereals.
    The main constituent of muesli.

Rice

1   Whole grain

Two main types:
(*a*) Short grain;
(*b*) Long grain.

Use:

(*a*) milk puddings;
(*b*) as part of savoury dishes.

2   White (polished)

White rice has been milled to remove the outer layers of the rice, leaving it more refined but less nutritious.

Use:

as an accompaniment to meat dishes, e.g. curry and chinese food.

3 Brown – wholegrain (unpolished)

This whole grain rice retains its outer layer which is a rich source of Thiamine (a B Vitamin).

Use:
(*a*) as part of savoury dishes;
(*b*) as an accompaniment to meat dishes;
(*c*) in whole food, healthfood, and vegetarian dishes.

4 Rice – ground (powdered grain)

This is finely milled rice particles which are processed to give a fine grain white powder.

Use:
mainly used in milk puddings.

Sago (small grain)
This small grain cereal is the product of the sago plant.

Use:
milk puddings.

Semolina (crushed grain)
Semolina is made from the coarsely ground centre of the wheat grain. The powder is yellow/white in colour.

Use:
milk puddings and in some savoury items, e.g. gnocchi.

Cereals – flour

Most of the flour which is used in the catering industry is made from the most common variety of wheat – vulgare. The various types of wheat grain vary slightly in composition, some having a higher percentage of gluten (protein) and water. Flour is blended by mixing the different types of wheat to give the correct strength for a particular purpose. A strong flour with high gluten content is needed where a strong structure is required, e.g. bread. Flour is milled to refine it and make it suitable for cooking use. White flour is produced from a blend of wheat. Most brown flour is milled from strong wheat.

Brown flour – partly refined
In partly refined, brown flour 85% of the original grain remains. 15% of the bran has been removed. This improves the keeping qualities.

Use:
for bread, scones, cakes, and pastry.

Brown flour – (un-refined) whole wheat
Not refined. In whole wheat flour 100% of the grain is used.

Use:
for bread, scones and some pastry. Used particularly for whole food, health food and vegetarian dishes.

Wholemeal flour will deteriorate and lose flavour more quickly than more refined flours.

White flour

1 Wheat/soft

The strength is controlled by the particular blend. White flour is refined and only 70% of the original grain is left.

Use:
for sponges – Genoese or creaming method;
for short and sweet pastry.

2 Medium

Use:
for cakes made by rubbing in method or chemically aerated;
for heavily fruited cakes;
for soft yeast goods, e.g. Savarin.

3 Strong/hard

Use:
breads – plain and enriched;
for puff and choux pastry.

4 High ratio cake flour and high protein flour

These flours are for specialised cake and pastry use.
  Most pre-prepared mixes are based on these specialised products.

Use:
it is necessary to use specially proportioned recipes with both types of flour which are used with high ratio fats to give a consistent product.

Note: For catering use raising agents are added to flour at the time of cooking. Self raising flour is not generally used.

Cereals – Pasta

Cannelloni

Lasagne

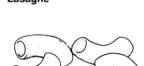

Macaroni

There are over 200 different shapes and sizes of pasta. Some are listed below.

1 *Canneloni*
2 *Lasagne*
3 *Macaroni*
4 *Noodles*
5 *Spaghetti*
6 *Tagliatelli*
7 *Vermicelli*

All pastas are made from flour dough.
The particular flour used is produced from durum wheat.

Spaghetti

Tagliatelle

Vermicelli

The dough is kneaded and rolled and then pressed into moulds or cutters to give the required shape.
The flavour can be varied by adding egg or spice.
The pasta may also be coloured, e.g. lasagne verdi (green).

Use:
(*a*) as an hors d'oeuvre, hot or cold, at the start of the meal;
(*b*) as a basis for a main meal course;
(*c*) served to accompany a fish, meat or poultry dish.

Sugar

White
1 Caster
The sugar is refined and sifted to produce fine, white crystals.

Use:
(*a*) baking cakes and biscuits;
(*b*) cold sweets.

2 Cube
Large and fine white granulated crystals are moulded by pressure into the cube shape.

Use:
(*a*) specialised bakery work;
(*b*) hot drinks as a sweetener.

3 Granulated
Refined from sugar cane or beet, the medium size, white crystals are produced.

Use:
As a general purpose sweetener. The most commonly used type of sugar.

4 Icing
This is granulated sugar which is ground finely to give a very soft white powder.

Use:
For all types of icing, for baking and confectionery purposes.

Brown
1 Demerara
Large pale brown transparent crystals.

Use:
(*a*) cakes and puddings;
(*b*) coffee as a sweetener.

2 Soft
This is a soft moist sugar which can be light or dark brown in colour and retains some of the natural flavour.

Use:
(*a*) baking, cakes and puddings;
(*b*) rich fruit items, e.g. Christmas cake.

Note: All white sugar is manufactured from sugar cane or sugar beet. Brown sugar is made from the syrup which is left at the end of the white sugar refining process.

Herbs

Basil
Has a flavour similar to cloves.

Use:
(*a*) added to sauces;
(*b*) the leaves are used in salad.

Bay leaf
Has a strong distinctive flavour.

Use:
added to meat and fish dishes, soups and sauces.

Bouquet garni
A mixture of herbs; usually parsley stalks, bay leaf, thyme and pepper-corn, wrapped in muslin. Commercially prepared packs are available.

Use:
added to savoury items, soups, sauces and braises.

Capers
Dried, pickled, unopened flower buds.

Use:
(*a*) added to hot and cold sauces, e.g. caper and tartare;
(*b*) in salads and hors d'oeuvres.

Chervil
Tightly curled leaf like a small parsley.

Use:
(*a*) for garnishing hot and cold savoury dishes;
(*b*) an ingredient in cold sauces.

Garlic
The bulb is divided into segmented cloves. Has a very strong flavour.

Use:
flavouring salads and savoury meat or fish dishes.

Horseradish
The root is used, grated or pulverised, and combined with cream. Pre-prepared sauces are available.

Use:
an accompaniment to meat; particularly roast beef.

Garlic

Marjoram

Sage

Tarragon

Thyme

Spices and condiments

Marjoram
A delicately flavoured herb.

Use:
for general use with meat and vegetable dishes and pizzas.

Mint
Varies in mintiness from gentle to strong-flavoured.

Use:
(*a*) for mint sauce or mint jelly to serve as an accompaniment to roast lamb;
(*b*) in salads or chopped for garnish.

Oregano
A light, delicately-flavoured herb.

Use:
added to fish and meat dishes and pizzas.

Parsley
The curled leaves are used.

Use:
(*a*) added to salad and sauces;
(*b*) the main use is for garnishing savoury dishes. Used either sprigged or chopped, raw or fried.

Rosemary
A delicate, light-flavoured herb.

Use:
added to lamb or chicken dishes.

Sage
A grey/green strongly-flavoured plant.

Use:
dried in stuffing or fresh chopped in salads.

Tarragon
A delicate thin blade-shaped leaf.

Use:
(*a*) for decoration e.g. chaud froid and to flavour vinegar, sauces and mustard;
(*b*) Added to chicken dishes.

Thyme/lemon thyme
The fragrant leaves are used. Very aromatic.

Use:
either dry or fresh, for stuffing, stews and herb sauces.

Allspice
The dried berry of allspice or the pimento tree. It smells like a mixture of cloves, nutmeg or cinnamon.

Use:
for savoury sauces and marinades.

Cayenne
Made from ground chillis or fully-ripened capsicum berries, it has a very hot pepper taste.

Use:
for meat and cheese dishes.

Cinnamon
Comes from the bark of a tree. It is sweet and gently aromatic.

Use:
for cakes, biscuits and fruit dishes. It is one ingredient of curry powder. Also used in mulled wines.

Cloves
These are the flower buds from the myrtle tree.

Use:
ground or whole in baking both sweet and savoury items. They are an ingredient of curry powder.

Coriander
The dried seeds are used, whole or crushed. It has a slightly lemon taste

Use:
added to curries and spicy dishes. Also used in the syrup of sweet dishes.

Curry powder
A mixture of hot spices and herbs. Usually made up of black pepper, cayenne, cinammon, cloves, coriander, ginger, mace, nutmeg, and turmeric.

Use:
powder or paste form, for addition to meat or vegetable curries.

Ginger
The dried, peeled root of the plant is ground to give the hot, sweet spicy powder.

Use:
in cakes, sweets and fruit dishes.

Mace
Comes from the nutmeg tree. The mace is the outer covering for the centre nutmeg kernel.

Use:
added to meat dishes and sauces; an ingredient of curry powder.

Mixed spice
A manufactured mix which is generally made up of caraway, cinnamon, cloves, coriander, ginger, mace and nutmeg.

Use:
added to cakes, biscuits, sweets, and puddings.

Mustard
The mustard seeds are used ground, whole or as a prepared paste. The colour of the mustard paste comes from turmeric.

Use:
(*a*) added to raw and cooked savoury items and dressings.
(*b*) served as an accompaniment to savoury courses. It is a condiment.

Nutmeg
The whole nutmeg is used grated, fresh or pre-packaged.

Use:
added to egg and cheese dishes, fruit dishes, cakes and biscuits.

Paprika
Ground sweet, red peppers.

Use:
the main flavouring of goulash. Used also in 'hot' savoury cheese or pasta dishes.

Pepper
Black or white dried peppercorns are crushed or ground for use, either freshly ground or pre-packaged. Black pepper has a slightly stronger flavour than white.

Use:
(*a*) as a general flavouring for all savoury dishes when added during cooking;
(*b*) also used separately as an accompaniment to savoury courses. It is a condiment.

Salt
A mineral – sodium chloride. Not a spice.

Use:
added to savoury dishes for general flavouring. Served separately as an accompaniment to cooked food. It is a condiment.

Tabasco
Made from a mixture of hot peppers – as for cayenne. It is very strong. Usually used in the form of a bottled sauce.

Use:
added to meat and fish dishes and savoury sauces.

Turmeric
A plant root from the ginger family, which is dried and ground. It gives a bright yellow colour to food. It has a slightly dull bitter flavour.

Use:
for colouring rice or other savoury dishes. An ingredient of curry powder. It is also used in pickles.

Vanilla
From the vanilla plants or pods, it is used whole, or as an essence.

Use:
added to cakes, sweets and puddings.

Fats and oils

Butter
Animal fat: butter is made from cream and consists of 82% fat, 15% water, 0.4% protein, 2.3% minerals, Vitamins A & D and added salt.

Use:
(a) for baking and general cooking uses;
(b) for spreading.

Lard
Animal fat: rendered from pork it is 100% fat. It is white and almost tasteless.

Use:
(a) for deep or shallow frying;
(b) combined with margarine in pastry;
(c) used in hot water paste.

Low fat spreads
Vegetable fats; have a low fat content, and added water which is blended with the fat and emulsified to prevent separation.

Use:
can be used in cooking to give low energy foods. Not suitable for frying.

Margarine – firm
Vegetable and marine oils: is of equivalent nutritional value to butter. Vitamins A & D are added during manufacture. Salt is also added.

Use:
used in place of butter for all baking and general cooking purposes.

Margarine – soft
Soft margarine has had a shorter processing time, which leaves it soft. Some margarines have up to 10% butter added to enhance the flavour.

Use:
soft margarine is easy to cream and spread.

Puff pastry margarine
Is made from:
stable liquid oil
hardened oil
soured milk
brine.

Use:
it provides a strong, thin fat layer between each layer of paste to give even rising. It is very plastic, tough and stretchable. Use commercially.

When cold, the puff paste can appear dull and lacks a crisp bite. Best used hot.

Shortening
Vegetable fat: 100% fat, it can be hard or soft. Soft used for creaming methods.

Used:
for specialised baking purpose, cakes and pastries.

Suet
Animal fat: a solid fat from the kidney region of the animal. Usually bought pre-prepared and packaged.

Use:
chopped or minced, for use in suet paste or stuffing.

Vegetable oils
Oils are fats which are liquids at room temperature. Vegetable oils are made from sunflower seeds, soya beans, walnuts, olives, maize, and groundnuts.

Use:
for deep and shallow frying and salads. Good oils have little odour, flavour or colour. Salad oils, e.g. olive oil, have more flavour.

Note: All fats and oils should be stored as airtight as possible in a cool place away from strong smells which may be absorbed by the fat or oil.

Fish

Quality Good quality fish can be recognised by:
1 A generally fresh, clean smell. Avoid fish which smells overstrong.
2 Firm, smooth and moist skin. – avoid shininess.
3 Plump, springy flesh.
4 Bright full eyes, and clear red gills.

Purchase Fish can be purchased:
1 Whole to be skinned and filleted and portioned.
2 Skinned and filleted ready for portioning.

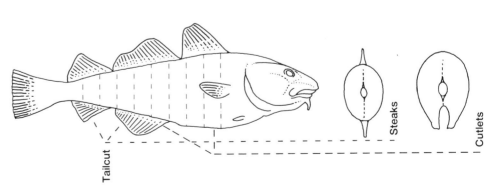

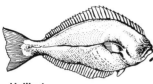

Halibut

3 Raw and pre-portioned with size, weight and quality control.
4 Pre-portioned and deep frozen.
5 Pre-portioned, ready-coated in batter, crumbs or sauce, and deep-frozen.
For whole fresh fish a calculation for cleaning waste and labour time has to be included in the cost calculation and the quantity to be ordered.
For pre-portioned fish the waste and labour cost have already been calculated into the purchase price.

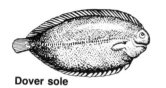

Dover sole

Storage Fresh fish should be bought as near to the time of use as possible. It should be stored in a fish refrigerator set aside for the purpose to avoid cross 'tainting' of flavours.

Fresh fish is held at a temperature of 0°C or 32°F. Frozen fish is held at a temperature of –18°C or 0°F

Lemon sole

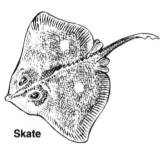

Skate

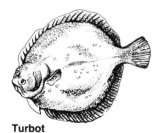

Turbot

Whiting

White fish

	Sea water	Fresh water	Flat	Round	Season	Use
Brill *la barbue*	√	–	√	–	All year	Fillets – poach, or shallow fry
Cod *le cabillaud*	√	–	–	√	Sept–Feb	In slices or steaks: boil, poach, steam, deep or shallow fry
Haddock *l'aigrefin*	√	–	–	√	Nov–Feb	As for cod
Hake *le colin*	√	–	–	√	June–Jan	In fillets or slices: bake, grill poach, fry
Halibut *le flétan*	√	–	√	–	July–March	As hake
Plaice *la plie*	√	–	√	–	April–Jan	In fillets: grill, poach, fry, steam
Sole, Dover/ lemon *la sole*	√	–	√	–	Dover: Sept–March Lemon: July–Feb	As plaice
Skate *la raie*	√	–	√	–	Oct–April	Poach, deep or shallow fry
Turbot *le turbot*	√	–	√	–	Sept–March	In fillets: braise, grill, poach, shallow fry
Whiting *le merlan*	√	–	–	√	All year (Best: Nov–March)	Whole or fillets; bake, poach, deep or shallow fry.
Carp *la carpe*	–	√	–	√	Oct–April	Whole: bake, braise, poach, fry.
Pike *le brochet*	–	√	–	√	Winter	Whole: bake, poach, stew.

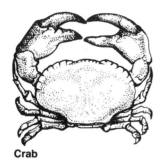

Crab

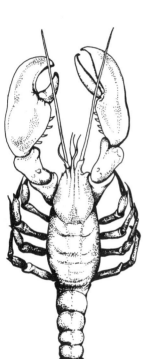

Lobster

Oily fish

	Sea water	Fresh water	Flat	Round	Season	Use
Herring *le hareng*	√	–	–	√	Jan–June	Whole or fillet: bake, grill, poach, shallow fry. Can be smoked.
Mackerel *le maquereau*	√	–	–	√	Spring & Summer	As herring
Sardine *la sardine*	√	–	–	√	Aug–March	Whole: grill or shallow fry
Whitebait *la blanchaille*	√	–	–	√	Feb–Aug	Whole: deep or shallow fry
Salmon *le saumon*	√	√	–	√	Feb–Aug	Whole, steaks or fillet: braise, poach, grill, or shallow fry. Can be smoked
Trout *la truite*	√	√	–	√	Feb–Sept	As salmon

Shell fish

	Season	Use
Crab *le crabe*	All year	Boiled. Main use in salads and hors d'oeuvres
Crayfish *l'écrevisse*	Winter	Boiled or stewed. Used in salads, and hors d'oeuvres
Lobster *le homard*	Summer	Boiled and served cold in salads and hors d'oeuvres, or hot in soups and hot savoury dishes
Prawn *la crevette rose*	Feb–Oct	Boiled for inclusion in salads, fish cocktails, savoury rice dishes and soup, and to decorate other cooked fish dishes
Scampi *la langoustine*	All year Best May–Nov	Boiled, poached, deep or shallow fried as a main dish
Shrimp *la crevette grise*	All year	As for prawn

Meat

Purchase   The purchase of meat is a large item of expense for the caterer. It is essential when buying meat to consider carefully
- the correct amount to be used
- the right joint or cut for a particular dish, to give the required flavour and texture
- the quality of meat required
- the amount of waste that is likely to occur due to preparation trimming and shrinkage during cooking.

Meat can be bought

1   On the carcass and butchered in the kitchen, provided that the staff, equipment and chiller storage are adequate. The overall purchase price will be cheaper but some parts of the carcass meat will be difficult to use up economically and the cost of the butcher's time must also be taken into account.

2   Ready jointed and then prepared for a particular dish by the chefs or cooks. The meat purchase price will be slightly higher but most of the meat purchased will be used.

3   Ready portioned, trimmed and cut to a stated weight, size, and dimension, e.g. steaks, chops, cutlets, pre-diced for stews or pre-sliced for braises. This method of purchase ensures uniform size and appearance, and portion control and cost control. The purchase price will be greater but the labour cost and trimming waste will have already been calculated into the portion purchase price.

This is becoming the most usual way to buy large quantities of meat for immediate use or deep freeze storage.

Whichever method of buying or preparation is used it is still most important for the cook/chef to recognise the cuts of meat and signs of quality and good condition.

As the price of fresh meat rises, substitutes are being developed and introduced. In manufactured products 'meat extenders' or 'fillers' are being used.

The product 'TVP' (textured vegetable protein) is a manufactured product made from the natural materials of soya beans or in some cases wheat, oats, and other vegetable sources. It is manufactured to take on the appearance and flavour of minced, chunked, or sliced beef, pork, lamb or poultry.

A 2 kg pack yields 6 kg when re-constituted by adding stock or water according to the instructions on the pack.

The soya protein can be substituted for animal protein up to 25%–50% to give a satisfactory effect in a prepared meat dish.

The right cut of meat for the right dish

(See √ on meat charts)

Good cuts of meat are suitable for roasting, frying, grilling and barbecueing.

Medium cuts of meat are suitable for slow roasting, steam roasting, pot roasting and braising.

Poorer cuts of meat are suitable for stewing, braising, pickling, stock making, and chopped, minced, processed, manufactured items.

Bacon   Approximate weight of a side 52 lb (26 kg).

Quality in bacon
Good quality bacon will:
1   be dry and not at all sticky;
2   carry a fresh, appetising smell;
3   have firm, smooth, white fat;
4   have clear pink coloured flesh.

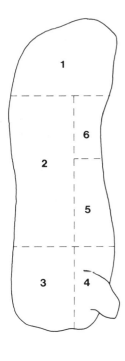

Curing and smoking bacon
All bacon comes from the cured flesh of pigs.
Curing is done by dry salting or soaking in salt solution to produce unsmoked bacon,
Further curing by smoking then takes place to turn green bacon into the more strongly flavoured smoked product. Smoked bacon keeps well and is slow to deteriorate.

| Item | Approx. weight | | Use | Good cuts | Medium cuts | Poorer cuts |
	Imperial	Metric				
1 gammon – corner/middle	14 lb	7 kg	Boiling, frying or grilling.	√		
2 back/loin	16 lb	8 kg	frying or grilling	√		
3 collar/shoulder	7 lb	3.5 kg	boiling or grilling		√	
4 hock	7 lb	3.5 kg	boiling			√
5 streaky thick	8 lb	4 kg	frying and grilling		√	
6 streaky thin					√	

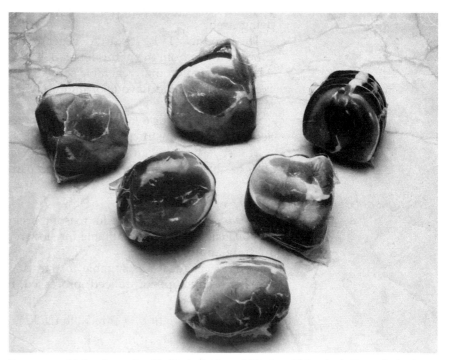

Gammon cut into pieces (by kind permission of Meat and Livestock Commission)

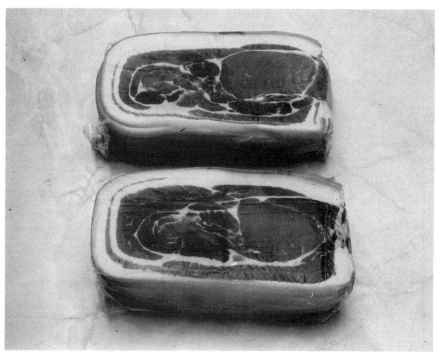

Thick streaky bacon (by kind permission of Meat and Livestock Commission)

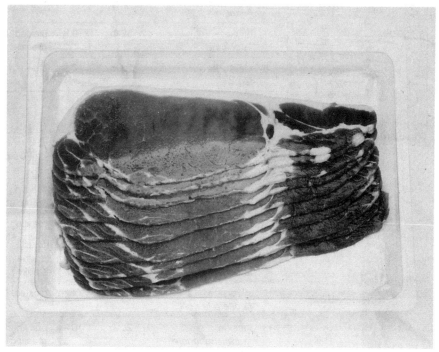

Thin streaky bacon (by kind permission of Meat and Livestock Commission)

Beef Carcass weight approximately 360 lb (180 kg).

Quality in beef
Fresh quality beef should have
1   bright red flesh with small white flecks of fat. The flesh should not feel 'slimy';
2   creamy yellow coloured fat which is firm, brittle and fresh smelling.

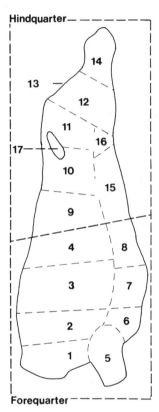

Forequarter

Item	Approx. weight		Use	Good cuts	Medium cuts	Poorer cuts
	Imperial	Metric				
1 neck/clod and sticking *le talon du collier*	18 lb	9 kg	sausages and prepared meat dishes			√
2 chuck ribs *les côtes du collier*	30 lb	15 kg	stewing and braising		√	
3 middle ribs *les côtes découvertes*	20 lb	10 kg	roasting, braising		√	
4 fore ribs *les côtes*	16 lb	8 kg	roasting, braising	√		
5 shank/shin *le jarret*	12 lb	6 kg	consommé, beef tea			√
6 leg of mutton cut *l'épaule*	22 lb	11 kg	braising, stewing			√
7 brisket *la poitrine*	38 lb	19 kg	pickled, boiled, pressed			√
8 plate *le plat*	20 lb	10 kg	stewing, sausages			√

Hindquarter

Item	Approx. weight		Use	Good cuts	Medium cuts	Poorer cuts
	Imperial	Metric				
9 wing ribs *la côte d'aloyau*	10 lb	5 kg	roasting, grilling, frying, steaks.	√		
10 sirloin *l'aloyau*	18 lb	9 kg	roasting, grilling, frying, steaks.	√		
11 rump *la culotte de boeuf*	20 lb	10 kg	grilling, frying, steaks	√		
12 silverside *la gîte à la noix*	28 lb	14 kg	pickled, boiled		√	
13 topside *la tranche tendre*	20 lb	10 kg	braising, stewing, roasting	√		
14 leg/shin *le jarret*	14 lb	7 kg	consommé stewing			√

Hindquarter *(contd.)*

Item	Approx. weight		Use	Good cuts	Medium cuts	Poorer cuts
	Imperial	*Metric*				
15 thin flank *la bavette*	20 lb	10 kg	stewing, boiling, and sausages.			√
16 thick flank *la tranche grasse*	24 lb	12 kg	braising, stewing		√	
17 fillet *le filet de boeuf*	6 lb	3 kg	roasting, grilling, frying, steaks	√		

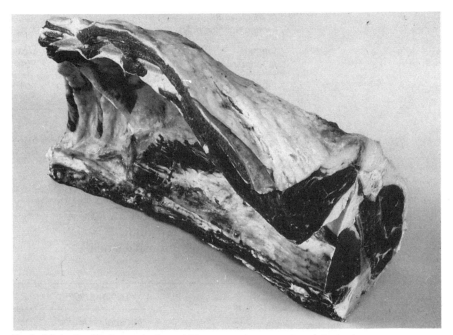

Beef sirloin (by kind permission of Meat and Livestock Commission)

Beef rump (by kind permission of Meat and Livestock Commission)

Offal (additional offal weight)

Item	Approx. weight		Use
	Imperial	Metric	
heart *le coeur*	2–4 lb	1–2 kg	braising
kidney *le rognon*	2–3 lb	1+ kg	stewing, soup
liver *le foie*	12–14 lb	6–7 kg	braising and frying
sweetbread *le ris de veau* (young animals only).			braising and frying
tongue *la langue*	3–4 lb	1.5–2 kg	pickled, boiling, braising
tripe *la tripe*	8–12 lb	4–6 kg	boiling, braising

Pork Carcass weight approximately 44 lb (22 kg).

Good quality in pork
Fresh, quality pork will have:
1 a firm non-slimy texture to the flesh;
2 white, smooth, and firm fat;
3 smooth skin and rind;
4 a clean, non-offensive smell.

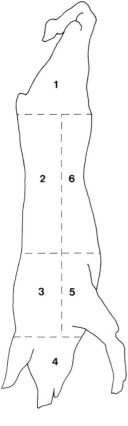

Item	Approx. weight		Use	Good cuts	Medium cuts	Poorer cuts
	Imperial	Metric				
1 leg: knuckle/fillet *le cuissot*	10 lb	5 kg	boiling and roasting	√		
2 loin *la longe*	12 lb	6 kg	frying, grilling, roasting	√		
3 spare rib *la basse côte*	4 lb	2 kg	pies and roasting	√		
4 head *la tête*	8 lb	4 kg	brawn			√
5 shoulder-blade/ hand/spring *l'épaule*	6 lb	3 kg	pies, roasting, sausages		√	
6 belly or breast *la poitrine*	4 lb	2 kg	boiling and pickling			√

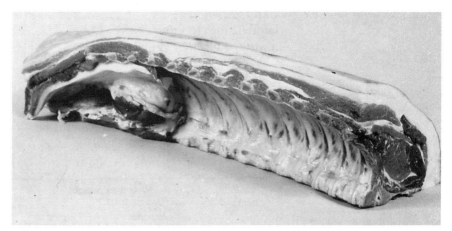

Loin of pork

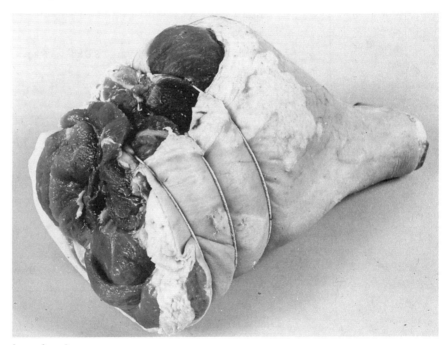

Leg of pork

Offal

Item	Approx. weight		Use
	Imperial	Metric	
kidneys *le rognon*			grilling and sauté
liver *le foie*	Approx. 6 lb	3 kg	frying and paté
trotters *le pied*			boiling and grilling

Lamb and mutton

Carcass weights:
lamb 32 lbs (16 kg)
mutton 50 lbs (25 kg)

Quality in lamb/mutton
Good quality lamb will have:
1   lean, dull, red, firm flesh;
2   clear white, brittle, flaky and hard fat;
3   a clean, non-offensive smell.

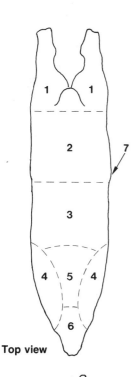

Top view

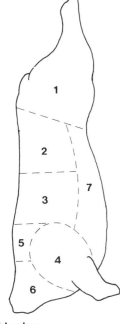

Side view

Item	Approx. weight				Use	Good cuts	Medium cuts	Poorer cuts
	Imperial		Metric					
	Lamb	Mutton	Lamb	Mutton				
1 leg (shank & fillet) *le gigot*	7 lb	11 lb	3.5 kg	5.5 kg	boiling and roasting.	√		
2 saddle *la selle* loin and chump *la longe*	7 lb	11 lb	3.5 kg	5.5 kg	illing, frying, roasting	√		
3 best end *le carré*	4 lb	6 lb	2 kg	3 kg	grilling, frying, roasting	√		
4 shoulder *l'epaule*	6 lb	9 lb	3 kg	4.5 kg	roasting and stewing	√		
5 middle neck *le cou*	4 lb	6 lb	2 kg	3 kg	stewing		√	
6 Scrag end *le collier/collet*	1 lb	2 lb	0.5 kg	1 kg	stewing			√
7 breast *la poitrine*	3 lb	5 lb	1.5 kg	2.5 kg	roasting and stewing		√	

Lamb offal

Item	Approx. weight		Use
	Imperial	Metric	
heart *le coeur*			braising
Kidney *le rognon*			grilling or sauté
liver *le foie*	Approx. 3–5 lb	1.5–2.5 kg	braising or frying
sweetbreads *le ris*			braising or frying
tongue *la langue*			braising or boiling

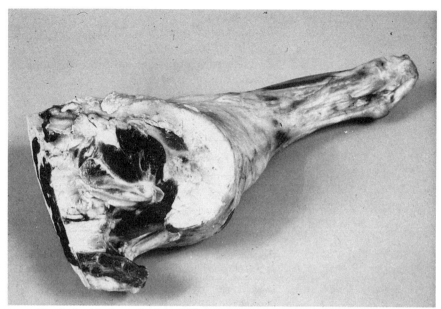

Leg of lamb (by kind permission of Meat and Livestock Commission)

Loin of lamb (by kind permission of Meat and Livestock Commission)

Poultry   *Good quality*
Good quality poultry will have:
1   plump breast and legs;
2   creamy white flesh without bruises or blood marks;
3   cleanly plucked flesh;
4   a fresh smell.

Chicken

| | Approx. weight | | | Number of |
	Imperial	Metric	Use	portions
baby *le poussin*	12 oz–1 lb	0.5 kg	grilling, pot roast	1
small *le poulet de grain*	2 lb–3 lb	1 kg–1.5 kg	roasting, sauté	4–6
medium *le poulet reine*	3 lb–4 lb	1.5 kg–2 kg	roasting, sauté	6–8
large *la poule*	4 lb–6 lb	2 kg–3 kg	boiling	8–12
fat hen *la poularde*	4 lb–8 lb	2 kg–4 kg	roasting, boiling, pot roast	8–16

Turkey

| | Approx. weight | | | Number of |
	Imperial	Metric	Use	portions
hen *la dinde*	8–14 lb	4 kg–7 kg	roasting	25–40
cock *le dindon*	12 lb–24 lb	6 kg–12 kg	roasting	35–70

Duck

| | Approx. weight | | | Number of |
	Imperial	Metric	Use	portions
duckling *le caneton*	3–4 lb	1.5 kg–2 kg	braising, roasting	4–6
duck *le canard*	4–6 lb	2 kg–3 kg	braising, roasting	6–12

Goose

| | Approx. weight | | | Number of |
	Imperial	Metric	Use	portions
gosling *l'oison*	4–6 lb	2 kg–3 kg	braising, roasting	12–18
goose *l'oie*	8–14 lb	4 kg–7 kg	braising, roasting	25–40

Fruit and vegetables

Fresh fruit and vegetables are a nutritious and colourful addition to a meal.

They are cheapest and best when in season, but are suitable for processing through freezing, canning and drying for later use. The fruit and vegetables must be processed when they are young and fresh and in good condition.

Fresh fruit and vegetables are graded for size and quality in line with EEC regulations.

All fresh items should be purchased as near to the time of use as possible in order to retain the quality and nutritive value.

Correct storage is essential to avoid bruising, damage, discoloration and deterioration. Items should be hung in nets or stacked on racks to avoid pressure, and kept in a cool, dry, airy store away from direct sunlight.

Fruit (fresh)

Item	Type	Quality: best when	Season
apple (cooking or dessert) *la pomme*	hard	firm and without bruise or blemish	Cooking: October–March Dessert: all year
apricot *l'abricot*	stone fruit	just ripe and not oversoft or bruised	May–September
banana *la banane*	exotic	firm, full yellow and unbruised	All year
blackberry *le mûron*	soft fruit (berry)	dark, plump and firm, (avoid squashed or dusty fruit)	August–October
blackcurrant *le cassis*	soft fruit (currant)	fresh, firm and juicy	July and August
cherry *la cerise*	stone fruit	fresh, firm and juicy	May–August
cranberries *le airelles*	soft fruit	plump and juicy	all year
damson *la prune de Damas*	stone fruit	plump and juicy	September–October
gooseberry *la groseille verte*	soft fruit (berry)	plump and juicy	June–August
grapefruit *le pamplemousse*	citrus fruit	large, juicy, with smooth firm skin	all year
grapes *les raisins/la grappe de raisins*	exotic	clustered in small neat, juicy bunches on a firm stalk	all year
greengage *la prune de claude*	stone fruit	smooth, plump, firm and juicy	August–October

Gooseberry

Fruit (fresh) *(contd.)*

Item	Type	Quality: best when	Season
lemon *le citron*	citrus fruit	firm with a glossy bright yellow skin: should be juicy and without too many pips	all year
mandarin/tangerine *la mandarine*	citrus fruit	skin is firm and glossy	November–March
melon *le melon*	exotic	skin is smooth and firm and the fruit feels heavy	all year
orange *l'orange*	citrus fruit	skin is firm, glossy and smooth and without discoloration	all year
peach *la pêche*	stone fruit	skin is smooth like velvet and unmarked by bruising or discoloration	July–September
pear *la poire*	hard fruit	just ripe, smooth firm skin: should be juicy	all year
pear – avocado *l'avocat*	exotic	firm but just about to soften: avoid oversoft or bruised fruit	all year – best in summer
pineapple *l'ananas*	exotic	skin is firm and without discoloration	all year
plum *la prune*	stone fruit	firm, plump and juicy; avoid when skin is bruised, discoloured or broken	August and September
redcurrants *la groseille rouge*	soft fruit (currant)	best when fresh, firm and juicy; avoid when squashed	July and August
raspberry *la framboise*	soft fruit (berry)	plump, firm and juicy	June and July
rhubarb *la rhubarbe*	vegetable stalk, usually thought of as a fruit	stalk is straight, firm, crisp, and pale, pinky-green	April–June
strawberry *la fraise*	soft berry fruit	just picked, full-red, firm and juicy	June–August

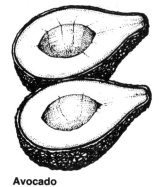

Avocado

Fruit (dried)

Item	Type	Use
apple *la pomme sèche*	dried apple rings or cubes	These and each of the following can be stewed and served alone or as part of compôte – hot or cold, as well as in tarts and pies.

Fruit (dried) *(contd.)*

Item	Type	Use
apricot *l'abricot sec*	whole dried apricots	
date *la datte sèche*	whole dried dates (usually stoned)	
fig *la figue sèche*	whole dried figs	
peach *la pêche sèche*	whole or sliced dried peaches	
prune *le pruneau sec*	dried plums	
currants *le raisin de Corinthe*	dried grapes	these and each of the following are used in baking, for inclusion in cakes, biscuits and yeast goods.
raisin *le raisin sec*	dried grapes	
sultana *le raisin de Smyrne*	dried grapes	

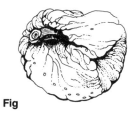

Fig

Fresh vegetables

Item	Type	Use	Season
artichoke (globe) *l'artichaut*	flower bud	tight and firm; the unopened flower bud and the heart are used	June–September
artichoke (Jerusalem) *le topinambour*	tuber	firm, crisp and unwrinkled; knobbly with white watery flesh	October–April
asparagus *les asperges*	stem	straight with tight unopened heads	April–June
aubergine *l'aubergine*	fruit	plump and firm with glossy dark purple flesh	June–October
beans (broad) *les fèves*	légume	young, plump and juicy	June–August
beans (French) *les haricots verts*	légume	straight, crisp, flat and stringless	June–September
beans (scarlet runner) *les haricots d'Espagne*	légume	as above	July–September
beetroot *la betterave*	root	firm, reddish purple	all year
Brussel sprouts *les choux de Bruxelles*	leaf	small, tight and bright green in colour	October–March
cabbage *le chou vert*	leaf	firm, crisp, with bright deep green colour	all year

Artichoke

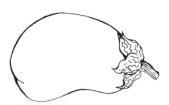

Aubergine

Beetroot

Fresh vegetables *(contd.)*

Item	Type	Use	Season
cabbage (chinese) *la salade de Chine*	leaf	crisp, firm, clear sharp colour	all year
cabbage (red) *le chou rouge*	leaf	firmly packed; strong colour	September–January
cabbage (spring) *le chou de printemps*	leaf	fresh, firm, and crisp	February–March
carrots (old) *la carotte*	root	smooth, firm and stumpy: avoid when split or soft	all year
carrots (new) *la carotte nouvelle*	root	smooth and firm	May–June
cauliflower *le chou fleur*	flower	firm and stubby with close flower head and sharp green leaves	March–December
celeriac *le céleri-rave*	root	firm and heavy in relation to its size	October–February
célery *le céleri*	stem	crisp and firm hearted	September–March
chicory *l'endive*	leaf	crisp and brittle	November–March
chives *la ciboulette*	stem/leaf	bright green and fresh cut	May–August
courgette *la courgette*	fruit	smooth, crisp and firm to the touch	May–August
cucumber *le concombre*	fruit	dark, shiny, firm, and crisp: avoid when soft	all year
garlic *l'ail*	bulb segmented	dry and firm with crackly skin	all year
kale–curly *le chou frisé*	leaf	crisp and with a strong dark colour	January–March
leek *le poireau*	bulb/stem	both white and green colours are clear and stem is firm	all year
lettuce – cos *la laitue romaine*	leaf	crisp and firm with no sign of wilting	June–September
lettuce – cabbage *la laitue*	leaf	crisp and tight	outdoor: April–September all year
marrow *la courge*	fruit	fully developed and firm but not over-hard	July–September
mushroom *le champignon*	edible fungus	firm, smooth and unbroken	cultivated all year; field – September and October

Chicory

Fresh vegetables *(contd.)*

Item	*Type*	*Use*	*Season*
onion *l'oignon*	bulb	firm, dry and compact with a crackly skin	all year; button in May–September
onion – spring *la ciboule*	bulb/stem	crisp: avoid soft wilted stems	May–September
parsnip *le panais*	root	smooth, firm and unblemished: avoid softness or brown discoloration	October–April
peas *les petits pois*	légume (seeds in pod)	pod is firm and juicy and peas are plump and crisp	June–August
peppers *le piment*	fruit	smooth, firm and crisp	September–November
potatoes – (old) *la pomme de terre*	tuber	best when firm and smooth-skinned, and free from blemishes	all year
potatoes (new) *la pomme de terre nouvelle*	tuber	skin is thin and rubs off easily	March–September
radishes *le radis*	root	plump and firm with a strong colour	March–August
salsify *le salsifi*	root	firm	October–March
sea kale *le chou de mer*	stem/leaf	crisp and firm	April–June
shallot *l'échalote*	bulb	firm avoid when soft or sprouting	September–October
spinach *l'épinard*	leaf	gathered for immediate use	August–November
swedes *le rutabaga*	root	small and firm	October–March
sweetcorn *le maïs*	fruit	well-filled and a good colour	July–September
tomatoes *la tomate*	fruit (usually thought of as a vegetable)	smooth and firm and just ripe	all year
turnips *le navet*	root	firm and unmarked: avoid when spongy	May–June
watercress *le cresson*	leaf	colour is deep and stalk is crisp	all year

Pulse vegetables *Beans.*
There are many types of beans, but red beans and white beans are the most commonly used.

Butter beans.
This is a large white bean usually served as a vegetable.

Haricot beans, white.
Can be large or small and used in soups and salads, or as a vegetable. The small beans are used commercially as the basis of baked beans in tomato sauce.

Flageolets – green.
These come from the French dwarf bean and have a delicious green colour. They are expensive and used only for high class items.

Lentils.
The split red lentil is commonly used for soup and vegetarian dishes.

Peas – whole.
Large and small. The large peas are 'marrowfat'. The small 'blues' are used in soup or as a vegetable.

Peas – split.
Either green or yellow. These are dried peas which have had the skin and husk removed. Used in soups, pease pudding, or as a vegetable.

Soya.
The soya beans are commercially processed to give soya flour or pre-pared 'meat like' products. The soya bean has a high protein value.

Pulses are dried seeds from the pods or shells of plants. All pulses are higher in protein, and provide a cheap, nutritious basis for dishes. They are used extensively in vegetarian diets. All pulses have to be soaked for at least 12 hours to replace the water and 'plump' out the items to their original size.

Can size and content

Can size	Weight of contents	
	Metric	Imperial
A10 old but still used	3.175 kg	7 lb
A10 new	3 kg	6 b 12 oz
A2½	825 gm	1lb 12 oz
A2	560 gm	1 lb 4oz
A1 tall	425 gm	15 oz
A1	300 gm	10 oz

There is some slight variation in size between manufacturers.

Pack size – dry goods	
Imperial	*Metric*
7½ lb	3.5 kg
10½ lb	5 kg

Wines, spirits, beers – alcoholic beverages

Wine, spirits, and beer have to be examined like any other commodity using skill, knowledge and judgement of the product when purchasing, storing or serving each specialised item.

An alcoholic beverage is a drink which is obtained by allowing yeast to feed on sugar in either a grape juice or a grain and water mixture. This produces alcohol and carbon dioxide, by a natural reaction which is known as fermentation.

A licence to sell is required by all establishments, where wine, spirits and beer are on sale on a permanent or occasional basis.

Main licences available

1 *Full on-licence*

For public houses and hotels where alcohol is sold for consumption on the premises.

Sales hours and conditions

Permitted hours in licensed premises in England and Wales are:
London area weekdays – 11.30 am–11.00 pm with a 2½ hour break after 2.00 pm. *Sundays* – 12 noon–10.30 pm with a 5 hour break after 2.00 pm. *Provincial area weekdays* – 11.30 am–10.30 pm with a 2 hour break after 2.00 pm. *Sundays* – as for London Area.

On Christmas Day and Good Friday Sunday opening hours must operate. These hours may be modified by local magistrates as long as the total number of hours do not exceed 9 in the provinces and 9½ in London.

Although drink may not be sold outside these permitted hours, a person may drink alcoholic liquor for up to ten minutes after the end of permitted hours.

2 *Off-licence*

For wine shops and public houses which sell wine for consumption off the premises.

Sales hours & conditions

Alcoholic beverages can be sold during normal business hours.

3 *Occasional licence*

For special functions.

Sales hours & conditions

Can be obtained only by someone who already holds a full licence.

4 *Residential licence*

For hotels, residential conference centres or holiday centres where alcohol is sold to residents.

Sales hours & conditions
Alcohol can be served 24 hours per day to residents.

5   Restaurant licence
For restaurants selling alcohol with a meal.

Sales hours & conditions
Alcoholic drinks can only be served when meals are being served.

Alcoholic beverages   *Beer*
- Ale – light/pale/brown,
  Bitter,
  Lager,
  Mild,
  Stout

Beers are produced from the fermentation of malted barley, flavoured with hops and other ingredients, according to type. They are supplied in casks, barrels and kegs for draught use, and in bottles and cans.

Use:
(*a*) for general refreshment;
(*b*) for service with snacks, meals and pub lunches.

Tied House: serves beer from one manufacturer only.
Free House: carries a range of beers supplied by different manufacturers.

Cider
- Still or sparkling.

Is produced through the fermentation of cider apples.

Use:
(*a*) for refreshment;
(*b*) for service with snack meals, buffet meals and pub lunches.

Wines
- Table wines/light wines

Wines are produced through the fermentation of grapes. They can be still or sparkling (fizzy)

Use:
Wines are chosen to complement the flavour of the particular food items which make up the whole meal.

Wine colour:
Red – with meat dishes
Rosé (pink) – with light meat dishes
White – with fish, starters, light meals and some sweets.

Wines can be:
sweet – with sweet dishes and fruit
dry (tangy) – with fish and light meat.

- Aperitifs:
  Bitters
  Vermouth

Wines which have been flavoured with herbs and spices.

Use:

They are used to tempt the appetite and start the digestive juices working.

- Fortified wines:
  Port
  Madeira
  Sherry

Wines to which a quantity of spirits (e.g. brandy) have been added. They can be sweet, semi-sweet or dry.

Use:

They can be used as an aperitif but are more usually drunk at the end of a meal to settle the stomach.

They are also used to flavour sweet dishes.

Wine producers

Country of origin	Region	Examples
France	Alsace	Riesling
	Bordeaux	Claret Château Margeaux Sauterne Graves
	Burgundy	Nuits St George Chablis
	Champagne	Möet et Chandon Mumm
	Jura	Château Chalon
	Loire	Anjou Rosé Muscadet
	Provence	Usually blended cheaper quality red and rosé wines
	Rhône	Château Neuf du Pape Tavel Rosé
Germany	Rhine (Hock)	Liebfraumilch
	Mosel	Piesporter
Italy	Sparkling	Asti Spumante
	Red	Chianti
	White	Soave
Spain	Red	Rioja
	Sweet White	Moscatella
Portugal	White	Vinho Verde
	Red	Dao

Spirits
● Brandy, Gin, Rum, Whisky, Vodka.

All spirits are produced by distillation. This is a method of separating alcohol from the other contents of 'wine' by means of evaporation and condensation. Spirits are concentrated in alcoholic strength which is described in terms of *proof*.

Use:
(*a*) for refreshment;
(*b*) added to coffee and sweet items;
(*c*) to flambé or flame foods such as steaks or crêpes.

● Liqueurs: Benedictine, Crème de Menthe, Chartreuse, Drambuie, Pernod.

Liqueurs are sweetened spirits. The particular flavour comes from the fruit or other flavouring materials which are incorporated during the production process.

Use:
Drunk with coffee at the end of the meal to help to settle the stomach.

Food science aspects

Contamination and food spoilage

Contamination of food makes the food unsuitable to be eaten. The contamination may come from natural deterioration of food or be transferred from one affected food item to another.

Contamination occurs when food is stored in the wrong conditions, e.g. too hot, too cold, too long or incorrectly packaged or when it is affected by harmful bacteria. If contaminated food is eaten it will cause a simple or more severe attack of *food poisoning* resulting in sickness and diarrhoea.

Cross contamination occurs through:
1   Incorrect storage of food items;
2   Poor cleaning of working surfaces between each preparation or service operation;
3   Inefficient washing of tools or equipment;
4   The use of already-soiled swabs, dish-cloths, mops and wiping-up cloths;
5   Failure to wash hands thoroughly after each job and after visiting the toilet or touching the nose, face or hair;
6   Careless movement of dust and dirt;
7   Use of already-contaminated water;
8   Failure to exclude domestic animals, vermin and flies from the working and waste disposal area.

Contamination and spoilage agents
1   Bacteria
Some bacteria are helpful, e.g. in digestion, but others cause damage, deterioration, and contamination in food. Bacteria are microscopic organisms found in air, soil, living plants and animals. They develop

rapidly in suitable conditions of warmth, moisture and food. They multiply and thrive between the temperatures of 6°C and 60°C (42°F and 140°F). Harmful bacteria are responsible for food poisoning.

Food care
1   Remove dirt carefully from all food.
2   Store foods at correct temperature.
3   Keep all dirt and air and warm moist conditions away from stored products or those in the process of preparation.
4   Use clean food handling processes.
5   Cook food at correct temperatures to kill harmful bacteria.

2   Chlostridium welchi
This harmful bacteria is found in:
1   The bowels of humans and animals;
2   Dirt and vegetables;
3   Raw meat.

Food care: as for bacteria.

3   Salmonella
This harmful bacteria is found in:
1   Human and animal excreta;
2   On hands;
3   Any food contaminated by excreta or hands;
4   Uncooked or lightly cooked food.

Food care: as for bacteria.

4   Staphylococcus
This harmful bacteria is found in:
1   Sores and open cuts or wounds;
2   Human nose and throat;
3   On skin and hands.

Food care: as for bacteria.

5   Yeasts
These are single-cell plants found in air and soil. The cells develop where there is moisture, warmth and food. Yeasts can spoil food through fermentation, e.g. jam and fruit. They are killed at temperatures above 100°C (212°F) and in high concentrations of salt. The cells remain dormant in cold conditions. Yeasts are used beneficially in the making of bread and wine.

Food care:
1   Exclude air from the food by covering or vacuum packing;
2   Store items in cool dry conditions;
3   Use items while fresh;
4   Use heat or de-hydration to destroy yeasts.

6   Moulds
These tiny plants grow on food, e.g. bread, fruit and cheese. They develop rapidly in warm, moist conditions. The spores are carried in the

air. Moulds damage food although some moulds are used beneficially, e.g. in blue Danish cheese and medicines.

Food care:
1 Exclude air from food by covering or vacuum packing;
2 Store goods in cool, dry conditions;
3 Use correct stock rotation to use up items while they are fresh;
4 Use heat or acid to destroy the moulds and spores.

Food handling guidelines

1 The food handler

Danger	**Care**
Check for:	
• condition of uniform;	change uniform regularly and wear clean items;
• cleanliness of hands;	wash hands between each food handling or production operation;
• cuts and sores.	cover cuts with water-proof dressing.

2 Receipt of goods

Danger	**Care**
Check for:	
• soil or dirt on food;	remove excess dirt before food is removed to the production area.
• uncovered or already contaminated food;	return food to the supplier where contamination is obvious, e.g. fly-blown.
• items which have already started to 'go off' or lack freshness;	check with supervisor – tell delivery worker – return goods to supplier.
• correct temperature of the transport vehicle or container for frozen foods;	return goods if the correct degree of coolness has not been maintained on the delivery journey.
• the hygiene of the delivery vehicle or delivery worker.	report the situation to the supervisor: return the goods to the supplier.

3 Storage of food

Danger	**Care**
Check for:	
• the storage temperature required;	store food items in the cool area set aside for them, e.g. dry store, refrigerator, deep freeze, and keep these areas at the correct temperature.
• inadequate or broken packaging or covering;	place food in clean containers or fresh paper or polythene packing container.

• 'use-by-date';

return goods to the supplier if the 'use by date' has already been passed.

• damaged food.

return to the supplier and get a refund or replacement.

4   *Raw food preparation*
Danger
Check for:
• preparation not being carried out in the area set aside for a particular item, e.g. vegetable preparation;
• foods left uncovered between each stage of the preparation process;
• prepared foods left standing in the warm production area between stages in the preparation process.

Care

prepare each item in the correct place, e.g. vegetables in the vegetable preparation area, sweets and pastry in the pastry area.
keep foods covered at all times by lids, clean fabric, transparent cling-film, or polythene sheet.
put foods in the process of preparation onto a trolley which can be wheeled into the cool store or refrigerator room.

5   *Cooking*
Danger
Check for:
• the use of correct time and temperature for cooking each different item;
• cleanliness of the cooking containers;
• foods which are cooked too far in advance of the service time;

Care

apply the correct cooking method, time and temperature to food to kill off harmful bacteria.
check cooking containers and re-wash before use if necessary.
time the cooking of food carefully to meet the service time or pre-prepare food and blast-chill it ready to re-heat quickly as needed, e.g. in a micro-wave oven.

6   *Food service*
Danger
Check for:
• food which is left uncovered;
• food which is requested from the kitchen too far in advance of customers' needs;
• food standing for long periods in warm, moist, dangerous conditions;
• slovenly food handlers, e.g. not using food service aids like tongs;

Care

keep food covered at all times.
be clear when ordering food from the kitchen – tell them when it will be needed.
keep food either very hot or very cool to prevent the development of food poisoning agents.
use food service aids and tools correctly at all times.

• dirty utensils or surfaces	wash utensils and surfaces with hot, soapy water, rinse and dry well.

7   Cleaning in the production or service area

Danger	**Care**
Check for:	
• dirty surfaces;	wash surfaces thoroughly and regularly using clean water and clean swabs.
• badly washed utensils and equipment;	as above.
• servery equipment not washed between use on different food items;	check that all utensils are washed between use on different kinds of food.

8   Waste disposal

Danger	**Care**
Check for:	
• food waste left lying about the service area;	clear food waste immediately into a bin sac or waste disposal unit.
• overflowing waste disposal sacks or bins;	place waste carefully into sacs or bins – never fill either more than ⅔ full.
• careless emptying of waste bins or incorrect sealing of bin sacks;	take care when emptying bins. Pick up any dropped waste and swill the affected floor area thoroughly.

Food hygiene (General) Regulations 1970

These regulations apply to any place where food is served to the public. They cover:
1   The need to provide and keep premises in a hygienic condition.
2   The responsibility to keep all food handlers, tools and equipment clean.
3   The provision of hand-washing and cloakroom accommodation.
4   The temperature and conditions in which food should be stored.

Food preservation

The aim of preservation is to produce conditions in which contamination and food spoilage will not occur, while at the same time retaining the nutrients, colour, flavour, texture and appearance of food items for use at a later time.

1   AFD – accelerated freeze dry
The food is quick frozen until small ice crystals are formed. These are removed through vapourising as the food is heated in a vacuum. This is a very efficient method which causes little damage to the food.

2   Drying
The moisture is driven off or drained off through evaporation leaving

the food in dry form. As moisture is one of the main requirements for the development of all spoilage agents the new dry environment stops their growth and avoids food spoilage. The drying is done by the spray drying or hot-air bed drying process. The water is replaced when the dry items are soaked, mixed and re-constituted before use.

3 Canning/sterilising

Uses heat to destroy micro-organisms and enzyme activity. Foods are surrounded in the can by a sugar syrup or salt liquid. The liquid and food fill all the space, so excluding air from inside the can. The can is sealed and passed first through boiling water to sterilise the can and then through chilled water to stop the cooking/sterilising process and cool the can. This process destroys the heat sensitive vitamins B1 and C.

4 Chilling

Makes food safe for short periods of time. Pre-prepared foods chilled down to 3°C (38°F) can be held for up to 5 days. It causes little damage to food and assists early preparation of food items. Use of a blast chiller will quickly reduce the food temperature to a safe level (*see* Food Production Systems, page 97). Chilled items must *always* be brought quickly up to use temperature and served immediately. *Never* re-chill or re-freeze.

5 Freezing/deep freezing

The severe reduction of temperature slows down the activity of the micro-organisms (some will be destroyed altogether) and stops deterioration. Foods can be quickly brought down to below freezing point using a blast freezer. Once the temperature is raised during thawing the growth and multiplication of the spoilage agents starts up again. Freezing therefore only preserves the food temporarily. Thawing must be done slowly and thoroughly. Items which have been deep frozen and thawed must *never* be deep frozen for a second time. Some structural damage does occur to the food.

6 Vacuum sealing

Operates by sucking all air out of the pack before it is sealed, thus cutting out any air-born yeasts, moulds or bacteria and creating cool, dry, airless conditions quite unsuitable for the development of spoilage agents.

7 Pickling

Involves the use of chemical preservatives such as salt or vinegar. The salt solution or vinegar is introduced into the food's cell structure through 'osmosis' and provides an environment in the food which is quite unsuitable for the growth and development of the food spoilage agents.

Raising agents

In order to make any bread or cake mix rise, air or gas has to be incorporated into it before baking takes place. With chemical raising agents the gas expands on heating and helps the product to rise. Where air is included into the item through whisking, beating or folding (mechanical means) the shape of the finished product is held firm when the protein ingredient sets (coagulates) during the cooking process to provide a framework.

Any mixture which is going to rise must be able to stretch and hold its shape when it has risen. Gluten forms when water is added to wheat flour. This gluten made up from proteins becomes elastic and stretchy when kneaded and sets or coagulates when cooked, to hold the shape of the item.

Air

Air can be trapped into food by mechanical means of:
1. creaming; e.g. in sponge cakes where the fat and sugar are beaten together;
2. Folding-in; e.g. flaky and puff pastry, where the paste is rolled, folded and rested to build up thin layers of pastry with air trapped between the layers;
3. Rubbing in, e.g. in short crust pastry or rubbed in cake mixes where air is trapped as the fat is rubbed into the flour;
4. Whisking; e.g. whisked sponge and meringue or whisked egg based items. (*see* Eggs below.)

Eggs

Eggs act as a raising agent through their ability to trap and hold air when whisked or beaten. Egg white can hold up to seven times its own volume of air. Whole eggs are capable of trapping a large volume of air.

Bicarbonate of soda

This is a chemical raising agent which works together with an acid – usually cream of tartar – to cause a chemical reaction (the production of carbon dioxide, CO_2) within the food which causes it to rise during cooking. It is an alkali. Cream of tartar: an acid used to counteract the soda taste of bicarbonate and to complete the chemical reaction which leads to raising. (Use 1 part of bicarbonate of soda to 2 parts of cream of tartar.)

Baking powder

This is the commercially mixed product which combines:
1. bicarbonate of soda
2. acid calcium phosphate-acid sodium pyrophosphate.
3. starch, e.g. rice starch. The starch is added to absorb moisture from the atmosphere and so hold off the reaction to create CO_2 until baking occurs.

Yeast

Yeast acts like a chemical raising agent, but it is a natural agent. Both fresh yeast and dried yeast are cultivated and manufactured for baking use. Yeast acts as a raising agent by giving off CO_2 and alcohol during fermentation. Fermentation takes place when:
1. temperature is between 25°C–29°C (77°F–84°F) although a 'cold rise' can be achieved at a lower temperature;
2. there is a suitable source of food, e.g. flour and sugar;
3. when there is moisture present.
Yeast activity is halted during cooking.

Nutrition

Diet

Good diet is a basic requirement of good health. It assists in the growth, warmth, maintenance and repair of the living body. It is necessary to balance the food eaten with the basic energy and activity it has to support at any stage of growth or age.

A sensible diet includes a small quantity of all foods available. It is dangerous to exclude any food from the diet completely or to live on a single food item.

There is a growing interest in the achievement of sound nutrition, as sensible eating contributes greatly to the prevention of illness and the maintenance of good body shape and condition.

Food values

There are three main categories of food – carbohydrates, proteins, and fats.

Carbohydrates   Carbohydrates are necessary to provide the fuel and energy to support physical activity. They also assist in the assimilation of other foods. They generate heat for warmth.

Sources: Cereal products, e.g. bread, cakes, potatoes, root vegetables, sugar, sweets, fresh fruit, beer and chocolate.

Proteins   They are essential for body building and repair of the soft tissue of the body. The nutritive value of proteins can be affected by over-cooking. Protein is made up of a collection of amino-acids.

Sources: Fish, poultry, meat, dairy products, grains, vegetables and pulses.

Fats   Fats provide a reserve source of energy. They have a supply of fat soluble vitamins. Fats surround and protect the body organs from damage and protect the skin from dryness. Deposits of excess fat can squeeze the body organs and put a strain on all the body systems. Fats provide warmth for the body.

Sources: Meat, oily fish, nuts, eggs, vegetables, butter, lard, margarine, vegetable oil.

These three main nutrients should be balanced in the daily diet.
50% of daily diet being carbohydrate
10% of daily diet being protein
30–40% of daily diet being fat
+ liquid.

Minerals, vitamins and water make up the other essential part of the diet. Minerals play an essential part in the control of all the body processes. Some of the food eaten should be fibrous, e.g. bran, brown bread and fresh vegetables to provide roughage. The roughage and water combine to help the waste parts of food to pass quickly through the body and to be expelled easily.

Minerals

Calcium
Essential for building and maintenance of bones and teeth. Important for heart regulation and nerves. Lack of calcium will lead to weak bones.

Sources: Milk, cheese, almonds, broccoli, wholegrains, yoghourt.

Chlorine
Important in metabolism where it works with sodium.

Sources: Celery, lettuce, spinach, tomatoes, salt.

Copper
Helps in the use of iron in the body. Plays a part in giving hair colour. Lack of copper can lead to greyness or hair loss.

Sources: Cabbage, nuts, liver, kidney, whole grains, poultry.

Fluorine
Helps prevent tooth decay

Diagram of food values

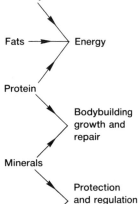

Carbohydrate

Fats ——→ Energy

Protein

Minerals → Bodybuilding growth and repair

Vitamins → Protection and regulation of body function

Sources: Fish, tea, seafood.

Iodine
Assists the correct functioning of the thyroid gland, which controls basal metabolism. Lack of iodine can lead to change of behaviour patterns, hair loss, dryness and wrinkling of the skin.

Sources: Salt, sea salt, seafood.

Iron
Necessary for the formation of red corpuscles. Lack of iron leads to anaemia.

Sources: Lean meat, offal, dark green vegetables, soya, and sunflower seeds.

Magnesium
Important in cell metabolism. Working with other vitamins and minerals it is necessary for the functioning of nerves and muscles.

Sources: Almonds, wholegrain, nuts, egg yolk, spinach, sea salt.

Phosphorous
Important for growth and maintenance. With calcium, it strengthens bones.

Sources: Meat, fish, egg yolk, cheese, wholegrains.

Potassium
Working with sodium it helps to maintain the balance of body fluids and is important for the action of muscles and nerves.

Sources: Potatoes, green leafy vegetables, citrus fruits, bananas, wholegrain.

Sodium
Works with potassium and chloride to affect cellular metabolism.

Sources: Green vegetables, sea food, water.

Zinc
Affects the protein and enzyme pattern during digestion.

Sources: Fish, beans, eggs, onions, wholegrains.

Vitamins   They are needed for the maintenance of general good heath. Lack of necessary vitamins can lead to digestive problems, depression, skin, gland and bone problems.

Vitamin A (Retinol)
Assists in the control of the growth of the skeleton. Helps good eye-sight and the repair of body tissue. Lack of Vitamin A can cause dry skin and early signs of ageing.

Sources: Carrots, apricots, liver, kidney, dark green vegetables.

Vitamin B1 (Thiamin)
Helps in the conversion of carbohydrate to glucose. Assists in the functioning of the heart, liver and nervous system. Lack of Vitamin B1 leads to shortage of energy and forgetfulness.

Sources: Wheat germ, lamb's liver, green vegetables, brewer's yeast, wholegrain cereals.

Vitamin B2 (Riboflavin)
Assists in the breakdown of food in the body and tissue repair. Lack of Vitamin B2 can lead to cracked and broken skin, especially round the mouth, split nails, and dandruff.

Sources: Eggs, cheese, milk, brewer's yeast, poultry, liver, kidney, green vegetables, yeast products.

Vitamin B3 (Niacin)
Necessary for mental health and the operation of the nervous system. Also helps digestion.

Sources: Sardines, chicken, kidneys, mackerel, lamb's liver, wholegrains.

Vitamin B5 (Pantothenic Acid)
Helps to avoid effects of stress. Aids the metabolism of fatty acids.

Sources: Yeasts, yeast products, kidney, liver, egg, bran.

Vitamin B6 (Pyridoxine)
Helps with the regulation of the nervous system and in the formation of antibodies and red blood cells. It contributes to keeping the skin looking young. Lack of Vitamin B6 can lead to anaemia.

Sources: Milk, wheat germ, wholegrains, nuts, mackerel, lamb's liver, poultry, bananas.

Vitamin B12 (Cyanocobalamin)
Necessary for the normal functioning of body cells, bone marrow and the nervous system. Helps to prevent early ageing.

Sources: Cheese, fish, milk, liver, kidneys, soya beans, egg yolk.

Vitamin C (Ascorbic Acid)
Important in the maintenance of health and beauty. Protects against stress and viral infections. Assists in the health of bone, skin, and cartilage.

Sources: Citrus fruits, blackcurrants, rosehips, sprouts, cabbage, potatoes, tomatoes, green vegetables, (easily destroyed by light, heat and cooking).

Vitamin D (Calciferol)
Necessary for the development and maintenance of bones and teeth.

Sources: Sunlight, dairy foods, oily fish, egg yolk.

Vitamin E (Tocopherol)
Promotes good circulation. Assists metabolism and helps to counteract ageing of the skin, respiration and sexual functions.

Sources: Eggs, olive oil, green vegetables, carrots, wheat germ, whole-grains.

Vitamin F
Reduces the chance of heart disease and keeps the skin in good condition.

Sources: Wheat germ, cod liver oil.

Vitamin K
Helps the normal blood clotting process and the functioning of the liver.

Sources: Eggs, milk, yoghourt, potatoes, cabbage.

Water   Two thirds of the body's weight is made up of water and it is the solvent in which almost every body process takes place both inside and outside the cells. Water is essential to the maintenance of life. It acts as a thirst quencher, a regulator and it also assists in the carrying away of waste matter. It is necessary to drink at least one pint of water each day, either in its natural state or as part of other drinks.

Stores and stock control

Food items and cleaning materials have to be bought in advance so that they will be available when required.

To prevent stock or store items from deteriorating they must be kept in the right temperature and conditions.

It is expensive to store items as cost will be incurred in the actual purchase of the goods and in maintaining storage space and low storage temperatures.

It is necessary for all items to be held securely in order to prevent loss through pilfering. It is possible to insure deep frozen items against loss due to failure of the freezer equipment.

Types of store:

1 Dry food store

To include:

1 Tinned goods.
2 Packaged goods.
3 Any non-perishable item.

Ideal temperature:
9°C–10°C (48°F–50°F)

Ideal conditions:
1 Cool and dry.
2 Airy and well-ventilated.
3 Fairly dark – sunlight filtered out by coloured glass.
4 Fly and vermin proof. Mesh covers in windows – no cracks.
5 Adequately shelved and equipped with bins, storage containers and space for cleaning.
6 Supplied with good, heavy duty scales and stores handling equipment.
7 Secure and lockable.

2 Cool food/kitchen store

To include:
1 Food items which are in the process of being prepared, e.g. left to cool before the next stage can be completed.
   This is a short term storage area.
2 Storing small quantities of food commodities, e.g. seasonings and herbs which are in regular use by the kitchen staff.

Ideal temperature:
9°C–10°C (48°F–50°F)

Ideal conditions:
1 Cool and dry.
2 Airy and well-ventilated.
3 Adequately shelved.
4 Fly and vermin proof.

3 Chill food storage

To include:
Items which have been fully prepared and are being held for up to 5 days before being served as part of the cook/chill system.

Ideal temperature:
3°C (38°F)

Ideal conditions:
A chill storage cabinet used *only* for storing items as part of the cook/chill system.

4 Deep freeze food storage

To include:
1 Raw pre-packed pre-portioned items, e.g. meats, fish, vegetables
2 Pre-cooked items, e.g. main meals, sauces and sweets.

Storage temperatures		
	°F	°C
Beer and white wine	50°F	10°C
Prepared foods	42°F	6°C
Dairy produce Cook/chill foods	38°F	3°C
Fresh meat Fresh fish	32°F	0°C
Frozen meat & Fish, frozen foods	0°F	-18°C
Frozen poultry	10°F	-23°C
Ice-cream	-20°F	-29°C

Note:
These temperatures give general guidance only.

Ideal temperature:
−18°C (0°F)

Deep freeze space is costly to maintain.

5 Refrigerator food storage
To include:
1 Storage of dairy goods.
2 Food items which have been prepared and are being held until service time.
3 Part prepared food items waiting to be finished. This is short term storage.
   A fish compartment, 0°C (32°F), may be part of the refrigerator facilities.

Ideal temperature:
4°C–5°C (40°F)

Ideal conditions:
1 Easy to get items out.
2 Easy to operate stock control and identify items.
3 Secure and lockable.
4 Adequately divided for maximum use and ease of access.
5 Easy to clean.

Ideal conditions:
1 Adequate, removable shelves.
2 Easy to clean and defrost at regular intervals according to manufacturer's instructions.

6 Vegetable store
Storage of fruit and vegetables – usually received on a daily basis and used almost immediately.

Ideal temperature:
9°C–10°C (48°F–50°F)

Ideal conditions:
1 Cool, dry, airy and well-ventilated.
2 Suitably shelved and with wall-hooks and slatted storage boards.
3 Uncluttered and easy to clean.
4 Access to an outer direct delivery door.

7 Cellar storage
The term cellar describes the area where alcoholic beverages are stored. The cellar must be:
1 dark, cool, dry and well ventilated;
2 kept at a temperature between 10°C–13°C;
3 secure and lockable;
4 suitably racked and shelved;
5 easy to clean. The cleanliness of all pumps, fittings and decanting equipment is of great importance in the maintenance of good quality and satisfactory flavour of all dispensed drinks.

8 Cleaning store
1 For all cleaning agents, e.g. detergents, sterilants.
2 For cleaning materials, e.g. swabs, paper towels, dusters, scouring pads.
3 Small equipment, e.g. hand brushes.

Ideal temperature:
9°C–10°C (48°F–50°F)

Ideal conditions:
1 Cool, dry, airy and well-ventilated.
2 Suitably shelved and with wall-hooks for hanging equipment.
3 Secure and lockable.
4 Provided with weighing equipment and issues area.

Stock rotation

Stock rotation will ensure that items are used while they are still in good condition. Just before a new delivery is expected, the items in the store will be brought up to the front of the shelves for immediate use. The newly received items will be loaded onto the back of shelves and will not be issued until all of the older stock has been used.

Storage and stock control

Manual systems

A manual stock control system will cover:
1 The checking, recording of all the stock received from suppliers as it arrives.
2 The recording of all items issued on a daily and weekly basis.
3 A periodic check of all stock held, e.g. weekly or monthly.
4 The explanation of stock loss through over-use, deterioration, over-weighing or theft.
5 Cross-check of the quantity of stores issued with the number and amount of food items produced, or the type and size of area cleaned.
6 A record of suppliers' names and addresses and usual delivery day or period.

Computerised systems

A computerised stock control system will hold a record of:
1 All items which are in the storage areas.
2 The date of purchase of each item.
3 The name of the supplier.
4 The purchase price of the items.
5 The unit price of the purchase.

Stock goods. As items are issued and recorded in the computer an adjustment to the 'total stock held' figure will automatically be made by adding or subtracting the amount of goods taken in or given out. At an agreed stock level for each item, the re-ordering of goods will be done automatically.

Perishable goods. As these items will be used almost as soon as they are received the computer will hold on record the details of quantity, quality and price of the items and refund or discount due. This information will be used to check against the claim for payment which will eventually be made by the supplier.

The issue of kitchen supplies will be based on the quantities already lodged in the computer record of standard recipes. The day's food order will be calculated by feeding into the computer the items to be produced and the number of portions required. Standard costing information can be used in the same way to provide a quick calculation of the selling price for each dish.

The computer will also indicate when too much stock of one particular item is being held and when 'use-by' dates have passed and goods must be used quickly.

For cleaning materials and agents it will be relatively easy to find the date when a particular item was issued and to judge how well it is performing, or whether the staff are very wasteful in the quantity or way in which they are using, for example, cleaning fluids or paper towels.

Storekeeper   Both manual and computerised stock control systems rely on the commodity knowledge and efficiency of the storekeeper who is required to feed the correct information into the system.

Buying   Before any food or cleaning commodity is purchased it is necessary to carry out product evaluation on a sample which has been obtained from the manufacturer or supplier. Several different samples of an item may be collected together and tested to see which particular one performs best.

Periodic product evaluation must be carried out on regularly supplied items to make sure that they are still working as well as expected and that no alteration has been made to the product which alters its efficiency.

Product evaluation   Products should be tested in the normal production situation or place of use. The tests will provide information about:

1   The quality of the raw ingredients or finished items.
2   The yield, e.g. how many portions are obtained, or what total surface area can be cleaned.
3   The cost of each food portion or particular cleaning operation.
4   The ease or difficulty of preparation and use of the particular ingredient or product.
5   Fuel consumption associated with preparation and use.
6   Appearance of finished food product or cleaned area.
7   Special storage requirements needed.
8   Storage/shelf life.
9   Size range of units of purchase.
10   General availability, delivery, and continuity of supply.

Patterns of buying   *Dry food goods/cleaning materials and agents*
Dry goods will be:
1   Ordered one week, one month or longer in advance of needs;
2   Ordered in bulk and held in stock until required. At this time they will be weighed into smaller amounts for use.

Freezer foods
Freezer goods will be:
1   Ordered one week, one month or longer in advance of need;
2   Ordered in bulk and stored until needed;
3   In the case of very large establishments, bought on a yearly basis and then delivered weekly or monthly to suit the rate of use and the amount of storage space in the food production situation.

Perishable foods
Perishable foods will be:
1   Ordered one week, one month, or longer in advance of need;
2   Delivery will be on a daily basis to supply fresh food for immediate use.

Food suppliers   *Cash and carry*
1   Bulk goods are sold at a discount.
2   The customer has to hve a card to gain entry.
3   Goods are paid for by cash or limited credit and have to be collected by the customer.
4   The cost of transport, e.g. van, petrol and driver's time has to be added to the cost of the goods when the price of an item is calculated.

To supply:
1   Dry food goods.
2   Wines and spirits.
3   Cleaning agents and materials.
4   Small equipment for food production and cleaning.

Factory direct
1   Goods are bought in very large quantities either by a company or a group of people who get together to form a buying group.
2   Discounts are large, therefore the bulk goods are much cheaper.
3   Goods once purchased can be delivered either to the group store or delivered at regular agreed times by the factory supplier direct to the place where the items will be used.

To supply:
1   Dry goods, e.g. flour and sugar.
2   Fats and oils.
3   Bulk purchase of ready portioned meat.
4   Freezer items.
5   Food production and equipment.
6   Cleaning equipment.

Local retailer
1   Offers a quick and convenient service being nearby.
2   Goods can be bought in small quantities.
3   Credit is usually given.
4   As the supplier knows the customer the service will usually be reliable and tailored to the individual needs of the customer.
5   Items will be more expensive as they have passed through more pairs of hands.

To supply:
1   Dry goods.
2   Fruit and vegetables.
3   Fish/meat and dairy goods.
4   Wines and spirits.
5   Cleaning agents and materials.
6   Small equipment for food production and cleaning.

Wholesale warehouse
1   Offers the advantages of bulk purchase prices while at the same time supplying small quantities of goods as required.
2   Wholesale goods will be more expensive than direct purchase items, but less expensive than retail.
3   The goods will be delivered on an agreed date as required by the production unit.

To supply:
1   Dry goods.
2   Fruits and vegetables.
3   Fish, meat and dairy goods.
4   Wines and spirits.
5   Cleaning agents and materials.
6   Small equipment for food production and cleaning.

Wholesale market
1   This is particularly good for *fresh* high quality produce which has spent the minimum time being transported from the grower to the market.
2   Prices will be good as only a few people have handled the goods at this stage.
3   The customers have to provide their own transport and so the cost of the van, petrol and drivers' time must be added to the cost of individual items purchased.

To supply:
1   Fresh fruit and vegetables.
2   Fresh fish, meat and flowers.

Bulk buying   **Advantages**
1   Bulk bought goods offer high rates of discount.
2   They offer a guaranteed supply of items of uniform quality.
3   When costs are generally rising bulk purchase goods can be a profitable investment.

Disadvantages

1 Bulk items take up a lot of valuable storage space which may be expensive to maintain, e.g. refrigerated space.

2 Money used to buy bulk items is 'tied up' and not free for other business uses.

3 Where there is a great fluctuation or possible drop in prices, money can be lost on stock held.

4 If not stored properly or used quickly enough bulk items will deteriorate and cash loss will result.

5 Unless secure storage is available goods may be lost through theft.

Quality control Quality control procedures are used in order to make sure that any item which is purchased from a supplier or produced in the unit is of acceptable, uniform, and constant standard. It also checks the 'value for money' of a product by making sure that the quality supplied matches the price quoted and that the grade of item ordered is the grade which has actually been delivered.

6 GETTING ON IN CATERING

> Discovering your interests and talents – knowing yourself
> Skills development and training opportunities
> Planning for job change and progression
> Applications and job interviews
> Moving away from home
> Catering – an international career
> Working for yourself
> Catering management and beyond

Discovering your interests and talents – knowing yourself

What kind of person are you?
To help you find out, write out four separate lists.

List 1
Describe your personality using a list of your own words.
Are you shy, friendly, active, lazy, willing, independent, adventurous, patient, short-tempered etc?

List 2
List your hobbies and interests and any full-time or part-time work.

List 3
List your achievements so far.
List your weak areas.
For example, your school record, or your work record.

List 4
Write down all of the things you would like to be good at – or aspects of yourself you would be prepared to develop.

Be honest with yourself.

Ask family and your friends what they think your strong points and your weak points are.

You will suit the Hotel and Catering Industry and do well in it if your lists include most of the points given below.

List 1
If you have a personality, manner and style which is:
- calm in a crisis
- caring about other people's enjoyment and happiness

- friendly and outgoing
- interested in the success and satisfaction of other workers – willing and co-operative
- strong enough to carry responsibility and to act alone when necessary
- adaptable and able to cope with a wide range of customers, a variable work-load and awkward hours of work
- energetic and enthusiastic
- able to enjoy variety, challenge and change
- good humoured and cheerful
- observant for detail and interested in achieving high standards
- honest and trustworthy
- confident enough to carry out work in public areas, e.g. bars, restaurants or reception.

List 2

If your hobbies, interests, full-time or part-time work include:
- mixing with other people of all ages, interests and backgrounds
- organising group activities
- preparing information about group activities
- finding out about new aspects of your hobby or job
- handling cash for a group or as part of your full-time or part-time work – using cash handling tills or computers
- handling food and drink items
- caring for others
- making or repairing craft items and finding new ways of doing things
- repairing and maintaining premises or equipment
- energetic physical activity
- an interest in travel and the life style of other countries.

List 3

If your achievements so far include:
- a good standard of general education, particularly in English and Maths
- suitable GCSEs or 'O' and 'A' levels to match entry to a particular level of course (*see* page 160)
- a good school report showing
  1 steady improvement, effort and willingness to work
  2 a good personality, able to mix with others
  3 a good range of school activities and hobbies
- a sound work record – good effort and attendance.

List 4

If you are interested in developing:
- weaker subject areas in school work
- sound relationships with others
- any weak areas of your personality, e.g. your temper, your patience, your concentration, your persistence
- a detailed and accurate knowledge of all aspects of Hotel and Catering work, through full-time or part-time training, on-the-job training, or craft proficiency recognition.

- your creative ability in both production and service aspects of Hotel and Catering operations.
- your physical ability to cope with a heavy work load and long hours of work.
- your ability to get maximum enjoyment from carrying out the varied work and giving customer satisfaction.

Now
1 Check the job descriptions on pp 15–21.
2 Match your interests and talents to the jobs which interest you and are available.
3 Check which course will lead to your chosen job on pp 161–67.
4 Decide how you will mix work experience and training.
Do you want to take a full-time college course or take a job which includes on-the-job training or part-time day release to a local college?

Skills development and training opportunities

All numbers refer to C & G Courses.

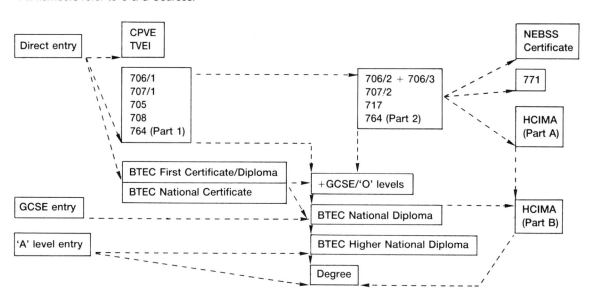

All of the qualifications on the chart are complete in themselves and will lead to a job in the Hotel and Catering Industry, at an appropriate level.

Abbreviations
C & G: = City and Guilds
BTEC: = Business/Technician Education Council
HCIMA: = Hotel Catering and Institutional Management Association
NEBSS: = National Examination Board of Supervisory Studies

Course	Body	Attendance	Period	Content	Entry qualification
700/1 Call order cooks	C & G	Industrial training scheme College attendance	6–8 weeks, all practical on-the-job training apart from 2 hours per week off-the-job training.	On-the-job: 1 practical fast-finish food production skills, practices, and procedures. 2 Health and safety practices. 3 Customer contact skills. Off-the-job: 1 Health and safety, fire and accident procedures.	None
700/2 Room Attendants	C & G	As for 700/1	As for 700/1	On-the-job: 1 Practical cleaning and services skills, practices and procedures. 2 Health and Safety practice. 3 Guest contact skills. Off-the-job: 1 Health, safety, fire and accident procedures	None
700/3 Food Service Assistant	C & G	As for 700/1	As for 700/1	On-the-job: 1 Food service skills, practices and procedures. 2 Commodities, tools and equipment. 3 Health and Safety practice. 4 Customer contact skills. Off-the-job: 1 Health, safety, fire and accident procedures.	None
700/4 Counter Service Assistant	C & G	As for 700/1	As for 700/1	On-the-job: 1 Counter service skills, practices and procedures. 2 Commodities, tools and equipment. 3 Health and Safety practice. 4 Customer contact skills. Off-the-job: 1 Health, safety, fire and accident procedures.	None

Course	Body	Attendance	Period	Content	Entry qualification
700/5 Bar Service Staff	C & G	As for 700/1	As for 700/1	On-the-job: 1 Practical bar service skills, practices & procedures. 2 Product knowledge, selling, tools and equipment, law. 3 Health and safety and hygiene practice. 4 Customer contact skills Off-the-job: 1 Health, safety, fire and accident procedures.	None
700/8 Cellar Staff	C & G	As for 700/1	As for 700/1	On-the-job: 1 Practical bar service and cellar work, skills, practices and procedures. 2 Product knowledge, selling, tools and equipment, law. 3 Health and safety practice. 4 Customer contact skills. Off-the-job: 1 Health and safety, fire and accident procedures.	None
700/9 Vending Services Industry	C & G	Industrial Training schemes. Work-based training.	To span a 12 week period (40 hours instruction)	On-the-job: 1 Practical vending skills practices and procedures. 2 Tools, commodities and equipment. 3 Display, presentation and promotion. 4 Health, safety and hygiene practice. 5 Customer contact skills.	None
705 General Catering Certificate	C & G	College, full-time	One year.	1 Food and beverage preparation and service. 2 Accommodation operations. 3 Reception. 4 Costing and communication studies.	Good standard of general education, particularly maths, English and science.

Course		Mode of study	Duration	Syllabus	Entry requirements
706/1 Cookery for the Catering Industry	C & G	College full-time, part-time, day or block release or approved work-based practice and exam.	One year. 300 hours. One year or equivalent block. According to individual agreed plan.	1 Methods of cooking. 2 The catering situation: commodities; tools and equipment. 3 Nutrition and menu planning. 4 Costing. 5 Health, safety and hygiene.	As for 705
707/1 Food and Beverage Service	C & G	College full-time, combined with other programmes. College part-time day block.	300 hours. 100 hours plus own employment experience.	1 Food and beverage operations. 2 The industry. 3 Health, safety and hygiene. 4 Service and pre-service procedures and cleaning. 5 Product knowledge. 6 Communications.	As for 705
708 Accommodation Services	C & G	College full-time, combined with other programmes. College part-time day/block.	750 hours. 300 hours plus own employment experience.	1 Principles and practice of cleaning and accommodation services. 2 Equipment and organisation. 3 Cost control and security. 4 Communications and industrial relations.	As for 705
709 Hotel Reception Certificate Note: This course is being revised and will be renumbered 720, Diploma in Hotel Reception and Front Office Practice	C & G	Full-time college attendance. Part-time day or block.	1 year. 1000 hours	1 Hotel reception principles and practice. 2 Book keeping and cash control. 3 General studies. 4 Practice in industry.	As for 705 plus individual college requirement.
764 Part 1 Cleaning Science	C & G	College full-time, combined with other programmes or part-time day/block.	240 hours	1 Principles of cleaning. 2 Cleaning materials, equipment and procedures. 3 Health, safety, security and hygiene.	As for 705
706/2 Cookery for the Catering Industry	C & G	Full-time college attendance. Part-time day or block.	600 hours or one year. 2 years or equivalent blocks.	1 Food production techniques. 2 Menu planning, nutrition, cost control. 3 Kitchen organisation and industrial relations. 4 Health, safety and hygiene.	705 or 706_1

Course	Body	Attendance	Period	Content	Entry qualification
707/2 Food and Beverage Service	C & G	College full-time, combined with other programmes. part-time day/block.	600 hours 200 hours plus own employment experience.	1 Organisation of food and beverage service operations. 2 Food service skills and procedures. 3 Cost and control 4 Law, supervision, and industrial relations.	705 or 707/1
717 Certificate in Beverage Sales and Service (Part 1)	C & G B1C/CM Distance learning material available	College full-time combined with other programmes. College part-time day/block.	120 hours 90 hours plus own employment experience.	1 Sale and service of alcoholic beverages: the principles and practice. 2 Personal and Supervisory skills	A good standard of general education or suitable work experience
764 Part 2 Cleaning Science	C & G	College full-time combined with other programmes. Part-time day/block.	240 hours	1 Cleaning materials, equipment, processes. 2 Organisation and supervision— human relations, industrial relations, work planning and supervision. 3 Health, safety, hygiene, and law.	764 Part 1 or 5 years suitable work experience (one year at supervisory level)
Work based training craft/supervisory	HCTB	A planned and approved schedule of on-the-job training.	As planned for the individual programme. Caterbase 'Open Tech'/ HCTB is available.	1 Limited skills programme. 2 Craft development programmes. 3 Trainer skills/supervision	Full-time approved employment or industry-based training scheme, e.g. YTS.

Course	Awarding body	Mode of attendance	Duration	Content	Entry requirements
706/3 Cookery for the catering industry	C & G	College based part-time day	480 hours	Has three parts: 1 Kitchen and larder, mise-en-place, design and display, food costing and quality control. 2 Pastry. 3 Advanced pastry. Theory and practice of pastry production. Food science and hygiene. Design, decoration and display. Quality control.	706/2
771 Organisational Studies	C & G	College based part-time day, or block attendance	240 hours	1 Costs, estimates, work organisation, quality control. 2 Group behaviour, industrial relations, human resource management. 3 Communications.	706/2 or appropriate craft and supervisory experience.
Certificate in Supervisory Management	NEBSS	Part-time or block college attendance or company sponsored programmes Distance learning material is available.	240 hours usually, covered in a one-year period for day release. P/T as above Full-time: 8 weeks.	1 Principles & practice of supervision. 2 Communications. 3 Industrial relations. 4 Economic and financial aspects. 5 Technical aspects of supervision, e.g. as relevant to Hotel and Catering operations.	Over 21 years old. Appropriate work experience or work sponsorship, or City and Guilds Craft qualifications.
Part A Professional Examination	HCIMA	Part-time college attendance or block release. Students must be in appropriate employment. While following the course correspondence material is available from Metropolitan College.	2 years	1 Business and supervisory studies. 2 Food and liquor studies. 3 Accommodation studies.	3 years full-time work in the industry. Advanced food and accommodation craft qualifications or 4 'O levels' GCSEs including maths & English. Suitable work experience.

Course	Body	Attendance	Period	Content	Entry qualification
First Certificate	BTEC	Part-time attendance.	Will vary according to individual arrangement.	Will include a combination of the following units: 1 Introduction to Hotel & Catering. 2 Introduction to food preparation and service. 3 The clean environment. 4 Hotel and Catering cost and control. 5 Food preparation. 6 Food and drink service. 7 Cleaning operations. 8 Reception skills. 9 Human nutrition. + work experience.	Evidence of a good standard of general education. School profile. CPVE. YTS. Or GCSE as requested by individual colleges.
Diploma		Full-time college attendance.	1 year		
National Certificate	BTEC	Part-time attendance.	Will vary according to individual arrangement.	Will include a combination of the following units: 1 Hotel & Catering administration. 2 The Hotel & Catering industry. 3 Hotel and Catering in context. 4 People at Work. 5 Purchase, cost and finance. 6 Housekeeping and cleaning. 7 Front office operations. 8 Food preparation. 9 Food & Drink Service. 10 Applied Science & options, & work experience.	BTEC First Certificate/ Diploma or 4 GCSE passes at grades A, B, or C.
Diploma		Full-time college attendance.	2 years.		

Note: Distance learning material is available through the HCTB and 'Open Tech'.

Course	Body	Attendance	Period	Content	Entry qualification
Part B Professional Exam.	HCIMA	1 Full-time college attendance (for those with 12 months industrial experience.	1 year	1 Foundation studies. The industry, marketing, management, technical operations. 2 Major studies: food and beverage management, financial management, manpower studies. 3 Elective studies. Options.	HCIMA Part A or BTEC National. Diploma (with specified units)

Part B Professional Exam. (cont'd)		2 Sandwich/college attendance (includes minimum of six months, supervised industrial experience. Correspondence material is available from Metropolitan College.	2 year		
Higher Diploma	BTEC	Full-time college attendance (includes supervised Industrial experience)	2 years for entrants with BTEC National Diploma 3 years sandwich for direct 'A' level entrants.	The unit system is continued on the same model as for the National Diploma. Option choices are available allowing particular specialisms to be followed.	BTEC National Diploma or usually 2 subjects at 'A' level. Alternative: 'O' levels/ GCSEs and 1 'A' level.
Supervisory/ Management	Company Training Programmes	In-company training plan as part of paid employment.	Usually 6–18 months.	1 Introduction to all departments. 2 Opportunities for supervision in all department. 3 Introduction to management systems, organisation, planning and control activity.	Entry at varying levels, usually 1 BTEC National Dip. 2 BTEC Higher Dip. HCIMA part B. 3 Degree.
Degrees	University CNAA	Full-time university	3 years or 4 years sandwich.	Individual universities and polytechnics put particular emphasis on certain aspects of the Hotel & Catering Industry. 1 Institutional Management. 2 Food Science/Nutrition Dietetics. 3 Accounting/Business Administration. 4 Design and use of catering systems and equipment.	Direct entry 'O' levels/ GCSE's plus 2 'A' levels or good BTEC Dip. Entry with some remission of time. BTEC Higher Dip or HCIMA Part B.

Look out for a new scheme for craft proficiency recognition/Caterbase
This is a modular programme which covers the areas of Food Preparation, Food Service, House Services, Reception. House Services Design, Decor, Senior Food Service Workers and Supervisors.

It offers flexible timing and programme length, and allows for 'add-on' modules to suit the individual's need.

Planning for job change and progression

Finding the first job

Look for adverts and job details in
- Central Hotel and Catering Industry Job Centre
  (Manpower Services Commission, 3 Denmark Street, London WC2)
- College notice board or careers advisor
- Hotel and Catering specialist employment agencies
- HCIMA (Hotel, Catering and Institutional Management) Hospitality magazine and appointment supplements
- Local Job Centre
- Local newspapers
- Trade magazines, e.g. *Caterer* and *Hotelkeeper*
- Direct approach to an employer, local or national.

What to look for:

Consider

1   The type of work you want
- food production
- food service
- bar/cellar
- accommodation.

2   The level of work you are capable of and qualified for and the duties to be performed.

3   The town or city where the job is. Do you want to leave home? Can you afford to leave home? Is accommodation provided? How much will accommodation cost? Will you be able to afford the time and the money to travel home if you wish to do so?

4   The size of the establishment:
- Do you feel happy working in a large unit?
- Are you at your best when working with a few people in a smaller working area?

5   The wage or salary:
- Is it an hourly wage?
- Is it a fixed rate of wage?
- What is the overtime rate?
- Does it include accommodation, meals, uniforms or other benefits which add to the wage value?
- Are there any fixed deductions?
- Is there a pension scheme? Does that matter to you at this stage?
- Is there a fixed holiday allowance?
- Is there an agreed rate of holiday pay allowed?

Finding the next job

The same basic questions must be honestly answered but as well as this the question of sensible promotion must be considered. It may be necessary to change job to gain promotion but vacancies may occur within your own working place.

You are more likely to be promoted internally or to move to another job if

1   Your experience has been thorough and good.
2   You have satisfactorily completed a programme of on-the-job training
3   You have undertaken HCTB training.
4   You have added to your qualifications, through attendance at college or correspondence, distance learning programmes.

Preparing for promotion

In order to be ready to take advantage of future promotion and career development opportunities it will be necessary to review the success of your working life so far.

1   Identify areas of technical ability or personality where you are strong; identify areas of technical ability or personality where you are weak; plan your career pattern around your strong points, while at the same time attempting to build up the weak areas through wider experience, practice or further training.

2   Consider the prospects:

● Where do I want to be in 5 years' time or 10 years' time?
● What kind of work and status am I aiming for?

3   Check whether your present qualifications and experience are leading to that goal. If not, carefully plan both training and experience over the next few years.

4   Explore the possibility of joining a balanced and varied company training programme which is designed to develop the individual's abilities while at the same time producing a valuable worker for the company.

Applications and job interviews

Applying for a job

Application forms

● Make sure all your information is accurate and up-to-date.
● Write clearly and check spelling – remember that the form gives a picture of you to the possible future employer.
● Type your form if possible.
● Check that you have answered all the questions asked.

CV (Curriculum Vitae)

The CV is a detailed list of all your information and is usually used instead of an application form. It accompanies a hand-written letter of application.

The CV should be typed and where a lot of applications are being made it is useful to type one copy and take photocopies from it.

It should contain:

1   Name, address, age, marital status.
2   List of work experience with names of employers, dates, job title and brief description of duties.
3   List of all qualifications giving name of school, college or professional body who awarded the qualification, dates and level of pass.
4   Details of any abilities or hobbies activities and interests which will be useful to the job, e.g. driving-licence held, typing, organising clubs etc.
5   National insurance number – if you have one.

Note: Do make sure that you have absolutely all of your important information written down. If in doubt ask someone to check it for you.

Letter of Application   A letter of application is a more personal document. It should be hand-written to give some idea of the applicant's ability to present information.

It gives a chance to state your reasons for applying for this particular job and to 'sell yourself' as being a most suitable person to hold a job.

The letter of application should be accompanied by the CV which gives all the factual information about the applicant. If a CV is not used, then this factual information *must* be included *neatly* and *accurately* in the letter of application

Approaching an interview

Preparation   It will consist of:

- Gathering together all your own personal information and reminding yourself about the dates and the detail of duties that you have performed.
- Checking the details of the job from the advert and the job description.
- Preparing the questions about the duties or the conditions to ask the interviewer.
- Collecting travel details to make sure of arriving on time.
- Considering how to behave to get the best result from the interview. How to be confident without being too 'strong' or too 'off-hand' and how to use your individual personality and style in the very best way.

The Interview   It will cover both information giving and information getting.

- Listen carefully to the details the interviewer gives about the job, the duties and the conditions.
- Consider whether these details match up with what you expected.
- Ask for more detail at any stage if you are in doubt.
- Be prepared to answer technical questions about the work and to explain how you would do it if chosen. Also answer questions briefly and accurately.
- Make sure that both you and the interviewer have all the necessary information on which to base a good decision before you leave.
- Consider carefully before agreeing to take a job. If in doubt ask for a day to think about it, although it is important to remember that other

applicants may be prepared to make a quick decision and so be given the job.

Moving away from home

Personal feelings

Good
- Excited by the thought of being independent.
- Interested in the adventure of moving to new surroundings.
- Proud of taking responsibility for yourself.
- Free from the restrictions of living at home.

Not so good
- Lonely away from family and friends.
- Frightened of being responsible for providing money for all your needs, food, clothing, accommodation.
- Lost in unfamiliar town and work setting.

Remember:
- Enjoy the good aspects and plan the sensible use of your freedom – remember there is no one to get you out of difficulty but yourself.
- If you have problems, think about them and try to find a sensible solution.
- Don't be afraid to write home for advice – parents and friends will be willing to help you if they know what you need.
- See your supervisor at work for guidance if a problem proves too difficult for you to solve alone.

The practical points

Accommodation *How to find it*
- Look in local newspaper.
- Check with estate agents.
- Ask at Department of Employment.
- Enquire at local council offices.
- Ask your new employer if they have any addresses.
- Enquire whether anyone at work is looking for a 'sharer'.

Rent
- Usually weekly in advance or monthly in advance.
- If you wish to leave your accommodation, the period of notice needed usually matches the style of payment, e.g. weekly or monthly.

Living-in
- An employer may provide a separate room or a shared room at the place of work.
- You will be responsible for loss or damage to your own belongings and to some extent for damage to the room and furniture.
- A deduction from your wages will be made to cover the cost of the room.
- You may be required to clean your own room.
- There will be rules of conduct setting out how you are expected to behave in the accommodation.

Personal Maintenance   *Food*
- Try to eat one main meal at work even if you are required to pay for it.
- Make an allowance from your pay at the start of each week to cover the cost of food. Eat plenty of fresh fruit, vegetables and milk to maintain your good health, particularly if your main food purchases are fast-food items.

Health
- Arrange to spend some time in outdoor activity. Fresh air is particularly important for workers who spend their time in stuffy bars, hot kitchens, and centrally-heated accommodation areas.
- Be active – exercise to create energy to cope with a heavy physical work load and to prevent feet, leg and back problems caused by standing for long hours in a hot environment.
- Sleep regularly and for reasonable lengths of time to refresh yourself after long hours of work and uneven shift activity. Sleep in a well-ventilated room.

Appearance
- Take great care of personal hygiene. Bath or shower daily and wash hair regularly. This is important for both health and appearance.
- Wash all clothes regularly, use the local launderette for batch washing and drying if space or facilities in your accommodation are limited. Send larger items to the laundry – check on the price before sending them and keep an accurate record of what you have sent.
- If you are wearing company uniforms, make sure that you prepare them for collection and laundering on the correct day to ensure a regular supply of clean items.

Remember
You have to plan all of these activities for yourself. Work out a sensible balance between working time, sleeping time and recreation time which allows you to get the most satisfaction out of all three.

Catering – An international career

Personal and practical points

Motivation   You must decide for yourself. If you want to secure a worthwhile career within the Catering Industry, you will need a combination of qualifications, professional expertise and determination.

You may be able to acquire the expertise needed by staying in Britain, but on the other hand you may discover that a wider international training and experience will offer you a much better career.

Benefits of industrial experience   Travelling, in Britain and abroad, meeting people of different nationality, background, interest and culture will be obviously beneficial towards your attitude to life and your maturity. Perhaps for the first time in your life you will have to stand on your own two feet.

The Hotel & Catering Industry is not conventional. It requires individuality, flair and first class expertise which can only be acquired through first class industrial experience.

Work opportunities abroad

It is not easy to find a job abroad. Most countries have similar large scale unemployment, or have very strict regulations concerning the employment of foreign labour.

Although you are free to travel and work within the EEC countries, you still could find local/regional restrictions.

Do not attempt to work abroad unless you have some qualifications and industrial experience to offer and obviously some knowledge of the language of the country where you plan to stay.

When considering working abroad, you have four options:

1   If you are already working in a catering establishment in Britain, ask your employer. He or she may have contacts abroad.

2   If attending a course at College, ask your Tutor or Head of Department. Many Catering Departments have their own exchange programme or contacts abroad.

3   Contact the Tourist Office and/or the Embassy of the country of your choice and ask for the names and addresses of the Hotels & Restaurants Associations (national/regional) and write to the president of these associations.

4   Purchase or borrow a copy of the tourist or hotels guide and write to the establishment of your choice.

Remember that when contacting an establishment in writing, you must follow this procedure:

(*a*) prepare a well presented curriculum vitae (details of yourself, your qualifications and experiences, and a recent photo)

(*b*) write clearly the reasons why you would like to work in that establishment, the kind of job you would like to have, the special expertise you have to offer (working, language) and how long you would like to stay.

Whether seeking a job in Britain or abroad, it is very important that you give a very good impression of yourself. This can only be achieved by producing a first class application letter, or by being very clear and polite on the telephone.

Type of job

Unless you are fluent in the foreign language, you must accept a craft level job until you are able to converse with the public and staff. You may find it to your advantage to attend a language school.

Wages

They vary from country to country and on what you are able to do.

By law, most European countries must adhere to wages regulations which include regulations dealing with room and board, insurance, income taxes, the number of weekly working hours, holidays, etc.

It is important that you ask for and receive a contract listing all these things.

Working conditions   They are similar to those found in Britain, with some exceptions.

Customers abroad are more demanding and expect higher standards of service, appearance and personality.

Be prepared to work and to deal with a variety of nationalities. If you live on the premises you could be restricted to being in by a certain time at night, no smoking or drinking in your room or overnight visitors.

It is well to remember that the employer is responsible for the welfare and safety of his staff whilst working or living on the premises.

Perhaps, at the start, the lack of the language and the new environment, working conditions, and food could prevent you from settling down for some time.

Problems at work   First try to solve them with your employer. If this fails, then ask for help and/or advice from one of the following organisations:

(*a*) local/regional Hotel-Restaurant Association

(*b*) local/regional trade union representative.

Private problems?   If you have any problem dealing with documents (passport), money problems, contact your nearest British Embassy or Consulate. If your stay abroad exceeds 2–3 months you are advised to register with the Embassy.

More personal problems could be sorted out with the help of social/cultural organisations such as the church (the Church of England is well represented abroad), societies or clubs. Your Embassy/Consulate will have the list of such organisations.

Accommodation   With the exception of large hotels and restaurants in big cities, most catering establishments abroad do offer accommodation on the premises or in a staff hostel.

If you have to find your own accommodation, you can contact:

• the local tourist office
• the university lodging office (if in the locality)
• the YWCA/YMCA
• church organisations
• the local newspaper

Do not leave Britain unless you are certain of obtaining accommodation on arrival.

Duties to perform   Besides technical ability and knowledge, perhaps the most important aspects the employers are looking for are motivation and adaptability to new situations.

An apprentice or a college leaver is still prone to making very costly mistakes. Employers do get concerned when they have someone who is not capable of discharging his/her duties effectively. It is most important that when applying for a job, you understand the nature of the work involved and you are certain you can do it well. You will be expected to start work on time and from time to time, to accept finishing after your normal finishing time. Remember a 'clockwatcher' never makes a good caterer.

Travelling   You have the choice of three ways if you exclude your own car/motorbike or hitchhiking which is not safe.

1   *Coach*: there is now a vast coach system in Europe. Most continental coaches leave from Victoria Coach Station in London.

This is the cheapest way to travel. These coaches generally do not stop, except for usual refreshment. If you have to travel through the night it is advisable to take a small pillow and a blanket with you. Some drinks and food are also recommended. Your local national coach service office or your travel agent will have the details.

2   *Railways*: There are no direct trains from Britain to the Continent. You will have to get on the ferry and then board your continental train the other side of the Channel.

First check whether your train will take you to your destination or not, and the names of the stops. Secondly, if you have to change, make sure that you have all the details as to where you have to change, the destination and departing time of your next train, and most important the platform number. Most European trains have a restaurant car which offers interesting food. But this could be expensive and if you are on a limited budget, take some drinks and food with you.

You will find in most railway stations shops selling food and drinks to take away. Railway restaurants on the continent are generally good and not too expensive.

3   *Airlines*: Although fast, this is the most expensive way to travel. There are however ways to cut the cost by using charter flights or other money saving schemes. Check with your travel agent.

If you travel by air you must make allowance for the time and the cost of travelling from the airport to the town, the railway or coach station. Also you will be restricted to about 40 lb on your luggage.

If you travel by rail or by air, check with your students' union whether there are special students' tickets at reduced price.

Before/on arrival   Once you have decided on how you will travel and you know the exact date and time of your arrival, write to your future employer informing him of these facts.

On arrival, and unless you have received other instructions, report to the reception desk, say who you are and ask to see either the Personnel Manager or the General Manager.

During your first week abroad, check with your employer whether you have to report your arrival at the police station, or whether you have any other such thing to do.

Get a map of the town and any pieces of information available, such as societies, sporting facilities, clubs, languages classes, etc. These can be obtained from the tourist office or the hotel.

You may find that you could be eligible for special reductions on public transport on presenting your student's card (if you have one) or your resident card. The railway or the coach station will have the details.

Documents and general information   Obviously your most important document is your passport. If you have one, check that it is still valid and if not, have it renewed. If you do not have one, you need to complete a special form which you can obtain from the Post Office.

Do not wait until the last moment. Allow plenty of time especially in spring and summer.

Do not lend your passport to anyone. The police might request it, and if so ask for how long. Keep it in a safe place.

Another document which you must have with you when working in an EEC country is Form CMI which you can get from the Department of Health and Social Security. This form covers part of the cost of medical treatment. But be sure that your employer has covered you for medical and hospital care whilst at work. If you plan to do some sport, take an additional insurance for this. Insure also your personal belongings before leaving Britain. The students' union can help you with your insurance.

If you are under medical care, ask your doctor to give you a medical note and also a list of the drugs you will have to take abroad.

If you are going to work in a non-EEC country, you will need a working permit which will be obtained for you by your employer. Keep this with your passport.

If you are planning to take money with you, allow just enough cash for the journey and have the rest in travellers cheques. You will be charged a small percentage for these, but if they are lost or stolen they will be replaced. Never carry large amounts of cash on you. Think about investing in a money belt.

The MSC has published a useful booklet *Working Abroad* which is available from your job centre.

Before you return to Britain

Check with your employer the exact date you are free to leave, whether you are entitled to paid holidays and any refund on income tax deducted from your wages.

If you registered with the police, the Embassy, etc make sure that they know of your departure. Do not forget to retrieve your passport and other documents.

Ask for a reference. In many countries this will be provided on an official form.

Working for yourself

Being self-employed.

Being self-employed is often the first stage in the process of developing your own business.

Nearly one-third of all working people are self-employed. It can be very satisfying to organise your own work, once the responsibilities of self-employment have been carefully weighed up.

A skilled or experienced worker can offer his/her services to individual customers, supplying them with – for example:

1 Food production services
● party and small function catering – hot/cold.

- sandwich rounds to offices and shops.
- cook/freeze food supply
2   Food service assistance
- dinner and drinks parties, shows/presentations
3   Drinks service
- bars for disco or dancing, parties or relief.
4   Cleaning and maintenance service
- regular cleaning
- special/spring cleaning
- home cleaning for removals
- small office or shop cleaning.

Note: When working from home or other people's premises check that the facilities comply with the Food Hygiene and Health & Safety regulations.

Job considerations   *How do you advertise yourself?*
- through friends – word of mouth?
- by reputation from one satisfied customer to another
- local paper/free sheets.
- local shops.

How do you book a job?
Use a standard job booking sheet laid out to suit your special needs. To include:
- name and address of customer.
- date, time, and place where work is to be done.
- number to be catered for.
- fuel and facilities available.
- parking available.
- food or drink choice.
- standard price.
- advance booking fee.

How will you be paid?
It's up to you to state cash or cheque and whether an advance booking fee is required.
    You must keep a careful record of all payments and expenses.
    To avoid delay in payment insist on payment on the day of the event or within seven days. The advance booking fee provides 'working cash' and helps your cash flow.

How do you calculate the charges?
Remember to cost all of your own 'admin' time as well as production time.
    Charges must include:
- labour
- materials
- transport

- staff costs
- admin costs/paper/postage/profit
  Profit is needed to enlarge your business, to invest in new equipment and to cover insurance, holidays, illness and slack time.
  (See p. 87 for calculation of profit.)

What records do you need to keep?
- record of all money paid out, with receipts
- record of all payment received
- record of all staff employed temporarily, to help you.
  Consult your local small firms service, the bank, or an accountant for advice on how to keep your records.

What about tax and insurance?
  You will be responsible for paying your own tax. Before you start trading ask advice from your local tax office about ways of budgeting to cover tax payments.
  You are also responsible for paying your own National Insurance contributions as a self employed person. Consult the DHSS for amount and method of payment and the range of benefits covered.

When will the business take off?
Plan your idea in detail on paper. Check all costs.

How can you be sure that it is a good idea?
Predict the rate of growth you can cope with on your own.
  Take your idea to
- the small firms service
- the bank
- an accountant
who will advise you from their experience about your chance of success. They will also give you help in improving your own basic idea.

Working for an agency

Hotel & Catering employment agencies deal with both
- full-time vacancies (usually short-term)
- part-time or casual vacancies.
The agencies' function is to introduce job seekers to jobs available.

How do you find an agency?
Consult:
- trade magazines
- addresses (See reference section of this book)

How do you select the right one?
  Get details – write or phone – from several agencies and compare rates of pay and type of jobs (the agency negotiates the wage rate with the employer).
  Most agencies deal with all aspects of the Hotel & Catering Industry, but some will be particularly useful for
- holiday work

- overseas work
- up-market jobs.

What do you have to tell them?
    Send full CV or give details of
- your age, training and experience.
- the type and range of work you wish to do.
- the geographical location you require, e.g. area or country, or a particular town, or range of mobility.
- the dates you wish to work.
- references from former jobs.
    You may be called for interview before the agency agrees to 'put you on their books'.

What do you have to pay?
Nothing
- For a relief job your employer pays the agency.
- For finding you a permanent job the agency makes a charge or may expect payment from your new employer.

What does the agency do for you?
    It matches your ability and availability to suitable jobs and helps you to find fresh employment when one job ends.

Do you have to pay your own tax and National Insurance?
    The person who employs you will deal with tax.
    Check whether the employer is paying National Insurance, particularly if the work is casual.

Can agency work lead to full-time work?
    It often does.
    When the job is made permanent the agency may make a single charge on the employer.

If you work for an agency are you covered for sick pay, or holiday pay?
Generally you are not since agency-negotiated wage rates will usually be higher than general wages. You have to save from this additional amount to cover periods of sickness or holiday.

Operating a franchise

Franchise is an idea often associated with fast food operations, but all types of business or separate aspects of a business can be operated on a franchise basis as long as there is someone to develop a particular franchise idea and work out the plan for marketing the idea.

What is a franchise? The franchise company works out an idea and in order to gain a large and continuous supply of finance to promote the idea and make profit for the franchisor, it allows individuals to 'buy in' the franchise. The individual franchisee then operates his/her unit using the name, decor, style and product items of the franchise.

What does the franchise offer?
- a well-developed and market-tested product
- a quality-controlled product based on standard recipes
- a centrally negotiated purchasing contract and list of approved suppliers.
- reduced discounted costs of standard products
- centrally planned advertising
- centrally planned layout of premises, and equipment.
- central supply of equipment with discounted cost for bulk purchases.

What do you gain by 'buying in' a franchise as a franchisee?
- a good product and a licence to operate under the terms and conditions laid down by the franchise company.
- cheaper quality-controlled purchases.
- the company's good name and a nationally stimulated demand.
- individual unit planning and layout.
- opportunity for extended credit purchase or hire of equipment, or discounted purchase arrangements.

What does the franchise company expect of you?
- That you maintain the set standards of the franchise company – the franchisor will inspect your operation and withdraw the franchise if standards drop.
- That you keep all aspects of the franchise agreement as laid out in the operations manual.
- That you pay the set initial amount to 'buy-in' to the franchise and make a regular percentage payout from turnover as agreed.

Buying in You will need to have access to an amount of capital before you can consider entering into a franchise agreement. However this initial amount can be much less than is required to set up your own full scale business.

Your own small business

General considerations

The law

What is involved?	**Where can you find help?**
It is necessary to check the up-to-date legal position in relation to:	Ask advice from a lawyer or solicitor
1 Employment of staff	
• employment acts	Department of Employment
• equality and discrimination laws	Department of Health & Social Security
• insurance and PAYE	Inland Revenue – local tax office.
• industrial relations law	
• wages	
Note A sole trader must notify the inspector of taxes that the business has been set up.	

2   Production, service and sales
activity
- food and drugs regulations
- food and drinks sales licence
- trading regulations
- VAT

Environmental Health Office
HM Customs & Excise

3   Working Conditions
- building and planning
  regulations
- fire protection procedures
- Health & Safety requirements

Local Authority Planning Office

Money matters
What is involved?
1   Starting cash
- equipment
- decoration and decor
- goodwill
- legal costs
- property/premises
- stock
- uniforms

Where can you find help?
Banks, small business advice
service, accountant, solicitor,
equipment manufacturers or
consultants, Department of Trade
and Industry Small Firms Service,
LEA development office, tourist
board, business friends.

2   Operating cash and expenses
- advertising
- consumable food and cleaning
  materials
- fuel costs
- interest on borrowed money
- own salary – staff-wages,
  National Insurance, uniforms
- packaging
- storage costs
- transport

3   Cash flow

(See p. 87, Costing.)

4   Profit
Profit is needed to assist in the
development of the business and
for replacement and expansion.

   Profit is your reward for the
hard work involved in running a
business.

   The required profit must be part
of the general *pricing* calculation.

(See p. 87.)

(See pp 87–8)

Premises and equipment
What is involved?
1   Purchases of premises and
equipment

Where can you find help?
Estate agents and trade journals

If you purchase you have an investment – the capital value of the property or equipment – but you must have either the cash available or security against borrowing to make the purchase.

You will be responsible for replacement and maintenance.

2   Rent/lease of premises and equipment
You have the property only for the duration of the lease or as long as you continue to pay rent.

The rent is a cost against your business and you are not making any contribution to an investment.

You will be re-fitting someone else's building. However, the owner will generally be responsible for the major maintenance and repair costs.

If the business does not 'take off' you can end the renting arrangement fairly quickly.

Lease/rent equipment will require regular payment. Lease/rent allows you to spread the cost of payment over a longer trading period.

Equipment will generally be maintained and replaced regularly according to the agreement.

equipment manufacturers
equipment suppliers
trade journals
local fuel boards (Gas, Electricity, Solid Fuel).

Staff
What is involved?
- the number required
- skill level needed
- duty hours to match the pattern of operating hours (F/T or P/T)
- wages and perks
Attempt to gain the maximum benefit from the minimum number of well-chosen adaptable staff.

Where can you find help?
(See p. 160, Skills development)

(See p. 27, Employment details.)

Style of business

Decide
- whether you wish to specialise in food or accommodation
- what type of customer you want to attract

- what volume of business you require, how many people are required to be fed or accommodated in a given period of time.
- what type of area you intend to operate your business in
- the type of building you need, size, shape, rooms, distribution of space.
- the maximum amount of capital available or the level of borrowing that is possible.
- the profit level that you require to support yourself and the business activity
- what you are best at – what can you offer that other people can't?

Review
- the potential number of customers in the area
- the cost of purchasing or renting property
- the ease of delivery and number of suppliers
- the possible competition in the area, for style, price, and efficiency.

Plan
- plan each stage of the operation in detail
- write down your ideas, check the legal requirements.

Organise
- setting-up activity
- operational activity
- checking and feedback

Make an operational plan and check all the details with a business consultant, government small firms service, the bank, an accountant or the tourist board.

Catering management and beyond

Those who wish to do well in the Hotel & Catering Industry must be prepared to learn continuously and build a good basis of both practical and supervisory experience and qualifications.

The qualifications – NEBSS, BTEC National Certificate/Diploma, Higher Diploma, HCIMA Part A & B, Degree (Sec. P Skills Development) give entry to supervisory and management opportunities in each of the main areas of food production and organisation, food and beverage service and organisation, commercial cleaning and accommodation services operations, and across all sectors of the industry.

As a member of a large or small company or as a freelance operator, other career possibilities exist using Hotel & Catering qualifications with the addition of specialised training or qualifications or experience.

Career development and extension ideas

Advising
- Business planning adviser
- Equipment consultant
- Health and Safety adviser
- Systems consultant – computers, front office, food and accommodation control systems
- Training and personnel adviser

Creating
- Decor design
- Food photography
- Floral design
- Function staging
- Hotel & Catering journalism
- Publicity and promotional material design
- Training material preparation.

Organising
- Central reservations and entertainments booking
- Conventions organisation
- Interior design and supplies
- Leisure services organisation
- Staff recruitment agencies
- Travel organisation

Selling
- Equipment supplies – large and small
- Entertainment and convention promotion
- Food and drink promotions
- Publicity – large or small company
- Function promotion
- Travel and tourism promotion

Technical operations
- Big building supervision and maintenance
- Dietician
- Equipment design and testing
- Food manufacture and distribution
- Food product and recipe development and testing
- Planning food production and food service systems.

In most cases entry to the particular specialised aspect of Hotel & Catering operations will be through job application to a suitable company who will then offer development training and on-the-job experience.

For detailed advice consult trade journals, job centre (professional service), relevant professional bodies.

Appendix 1 USEFUL ADDRESSES

Advisory, Professional and Trade Bodies

Army Catering Corps Association,
St Omer Barracks, Aldershot,
Hampshire GU11 2BN

Association of Domestic
Management,
22 Larch Walk, Kennington,
Ashford, Kent

Association of Home Economists
Ltd.,
307 Uxbridge Road, Acton,
London W3 9QU

British Federation of Hotel, Guest
Houses, and Self Catering
Associations,
Abingdon Chambers,
23 Abingdon Street,
Blackpool, Lancs.

The British Franchise Association
Grove House,
628 London Road,
Colnbrook, Slough, SL3 8QA

British Gas Corporation,
Rivermill House,
152 Grosvenor Rd,
London SW1V 3JL

British Motels Federation Ltd,
10 Bolton Street,
London W1Y 8AU

British Hotel, Restaurants &
Caterers Association.
40 Duke Street, London,
W1M 6HR

British Safety Council,
62/64 Chancellors Rd,
London W6 9RS

Catering Managers Association,
77 Fog Lane, Didsbury,
Manchester M20 OSL

Central London Careers Office,
145 Charing Cross Rd,
London WC2H OEE

Cookery & Food Association,
1 Victoria Parade,
By 331 Sandycombe Rd,
Richmond, Surrey TW9 3NB

Craft Guild of Chefs,
c/o Cookery & Food Assoc.,
1 Victoria Parade,
331 Sandycombe Rd,
Richmond, Surrey.

Electricity Council,
30 Millbank, London SW1P 4RD

Fire Protection Association,
Aldermary House
10–15, Queen Street
London EC4N 1TJ.

Food & Bev. Managers Assoc.,
Group Catering Executive,
Mecca Sportsmans,
3 Tottenham Ct Rd, London W1

Food Hygiene Advisory Council,
c/o Dept Health & Social Security
Alexander Fleming House,
Elephant & Castle,
London SE1 6BY

Guild of Sommeliers,
Five Kings House,
Kennet Wharf Lane
Upper Thames Street,
London EC4V 3BA

Health & Safety Executive,
25 Chapel Street,
London NW1 4DT

HMSO,
49 High Holborn, London
WC1X 6HB

Hospital Caterers Assoc.,
The Duver, 22 Conifer Close,
Lemon Grove, Whitehill,
Hants GU35 9BC

Industrial Catering Assoc.,
1 Victoria Parade,
By 331 Sandycombe Rd,
Richmond, Surrey TW9 3NB

Institute of Home Economics Ltd,
192–198 Vauxhall Bridge Rd,
London SW1V 1DX

Institute of Travel & Tourism Ltd,
53–54 Newman Street,
London W1P 4JJ

Institution of Environmental
Health Officers,
Chadwick House,
Rushworth Street,
London SE1 0RB

International Wine & Food Society,
66–67 Wells Street,
London W1P 3RB

Metropolitan College
(Correspondence College)
Oxford OX2 6PR

Commodities Information

British Sugar Bureau,
140 Park Lane, London W1Y 3AA

Butter Information Council,
2 Neville Street, Tunbridge Wells
Kent TN2 5TT

Catering Equipment Distribution
Assoc.
397 Bradford Road,
Huddersfield,
Yorkshire HD2 2QY

Catering Equipment Manufacturers
Association,
Suite 491, Park West
Edgware Road London W2 2QX

Coffee Trade Federation
69 Cannon Street
London EC4N 5AB

Dutch Dairy Bureau,
141/143 Drury Lane,
London WC2B 5TB

English Country Cheese Council,
National Dairy Centre,
5/7, John Princes Street,
London W1M 0AP

English Vineyards Assoc. Ltd,
Lamberhurst Vineyards,
The Ridge Farm,
Lamberhurst, Kent,

Flour Advisory Bureau,
21 Arlington Street,
London SW1A 1RN

Fresh Fruit & Vegetable
Information Bureau,
9 Walton Street, London SW3 2SD

National Dairy Council,
5/7 John Princes Street,
London W1M OAP

The Tea Council,
Sir John Lyon House,
5 High Timber Street,
Upper Thames Street,
London EC4V 3NJ

Education & training – Hotel & Catering Industry.

British Institute of Cleaning
Science.
87 Central Buildings
Southwark St. London

City & Guilds of London Institute,
76 Portland Place,
London W1N 4AA

HCTB, Hotel & Catering Industry
Training Board,
PO Box 18, Ramsey House,
Central Square,
Wembley, Middlesex, HA9 7AP

HCIMA Hotel Catering &
Institutional Management Assoc.,
191 Trinity Road,
London SW17 7HN

Institute of Meat,
Boundary House,
91/93 Charterhouse Street,
London EC1M 6HR

NCHEE (National Council
for Home Economics Education),
214 Middle Lane, Hornsey,
London N8 7LB

NEBSS (National Examinations
Board for Supervisory Studies),
76 Portland Place,
London W1N 4AA

Open Tech-Hotel & Catering,
Room E824 Manpower Services
Commission
Moorfoot. Sheffield S1 4PQ

RIPHH Royal Institute for Public
Health & Hygiene,
28, Portland Place,
London, W1N 4DE

RSH (Royal Society of Health),
13 Grosvenor Place,
London SW1X 7EN

BTEC (Business and Technician
Education Council),
Central House, Upper Woburn
Place,
London WC1H OHH

Wine & Spirit Education Trust Ltd,
Five Kings House,
Kennet Wharf Lane,
Upper Thames Street,
London EC4V 3AJ

Employment

Employers

Anchor Hotels,
Pier House, Strand on the Green,
Chiswick, London W4 3NN

Comfort Hotel, International,
167 Queensway, London W2 4XG

Concord Hotels,
7 Green Rd, Terriers,
High Wycombe, Bucks HP13 5BD

Crest Hotels,
Bridge Street, Banbury,
Oxon

Embassy Hotels,
Station Street,
Burton on Trent, Staffs, DE14 1BZ

Forces Catering
(Army, Airforce, Navy),
Local Recruitment Office

Grandmet Catering Services,
Banda House, Cambridge Grove
Hammersmith W6 OLE

Hamard Catering Management
Services,
Hamard House, Cardiff Road,
Barry, S. Glamorgan

Happy Eater,
16–18, Upper High Street, Epsom,
Surrey KT17 4QJ

Health Service Catering,
DHSS, Hannibal House,
Elephant & Castle,
London SE1 6TE

Instore Enterprises,
(subsidiary of Debenhams),
Bickler House, Tamworth Rd,
Croydon CR9 1XQ

Intercontinental Hotels,
(Grand Metropolitan Company)

J.L. Catering,
Glacier House,
London W6 7BT

Ladbroke Hotels, Holidays &
Taverns
PO Box 137, Millbuck House,
Clarendon Rd, Watford

John Lewis Partnership,
10 Clipstone Street,
London W1A 3DF

Merchant Navy Catering
Merchant Navy Training Board
Careers Advice
20–22 Prescott Street
London E1 6BD

McDonalds,
11–59 High Street, East Finchley,
London N2

Mecca Entertainment,
76 Souwark Street,
London W1

Norfolk Capital Hotels,
8 Cromwell Place, London

Post Office,
PP1.4, Room 354, Post Office,
Headquarters Building,
Martins le Grand,
London EC1A 1HQ

Scottish Highland Hotels,
98 West George Street,
Glasgow G2

Sutcliffe Catering Group,
40 The Mall, Ealing,
London W5

Swallow Hotels,
PO Box 8, Swallow House,
Seaburn Terrace, Seaburn,
Sunderland SR6 8BB

Travellers Fare,
PO Box 179,
St Pancras Chambers, London
NW1 2TU

Trust House Forte Catering/
Hotels,
20 Queensmere, Slough,
Berks SL1 1YY

Welcome Break,
(Formerly Motoross)
M1 Service Area, Leicester
Forest East, Leics, LE3 3GB

Wimpy International,
214 Chiswick High Rd,
Chiswick, London W4

FW Woolworth,
Woolworth House,
242/246 Marylebone Road,
London NW1

YHA,
Trevelyan House,
8 St Stephen's Hill,
St Albans,
Hertfordshire AL1 2DY

Hotel and Catering Staff Agencies

Angel Staff
52/54 Carter Lane,
London EC4V 5AS

Capital Catering Agency
95 Charing Cross Road,
London WC2H ODP

Chefs Centre
13 Frith Street,
London W1

Jubilee Catering Agency
25 Frith Street,
London W1V 5TR

(**Note**: The addresses listed in this Appendix are accurate at time of going to press.)

APPENDIX 2   REFERENCE INFORMATION

Alcoholic beverages

A Wine Primer, Simon,
Food & Beverage Service, Lillicrap, Edward Arnold
The New Wine Companion, Burroughs and Bezzart, Heinemann
Wine & Food Handbook, Tour, Hodder

Book-keeping costs

Book-keeping and Accounts for H & C Students, Grace & Jane, Holt
Catering Cost & Control, Paige, Cassell
Costing & Calculations, Hughes & Ireland, S Thornes
Money Guide, How to Survive the Money Jungle, Marie Jennings, TSB/Collins,
Money – The Facts of Life, W Reay Tolfree, Martin Books in association with Lloyds Bank,

Cleaning and maintenance

Accommodation Operations, Dix, Pitman
Commercial Housekeeping, Phillips & Jones, S Thornes
Hotel, Hostel & Hospital Housekeeping, Branson & Lennox, Edward Arnold

Food production

A Guide to Catering Organization, Julia Reay, S Thornes
An Introduction to Food Science, Kilgour, Heinemann
Basic Cookery, Martland & Welsby, Heinemann
Better Cooking, A King, Mills & Boon
Catering Food & Drink, Hilton, MacDonald & Evans
Chefs Compendium, Fuller, Heinemann
Cooking for Large Numbers, Julia Reay, Hutchinson
Commodities for Caterers, Lingard & Sizer, Cassell
Cuisine Minceur, Geurard, MacMillan
Deep Freezing, Cox, Faber
Elementary Food Science, Hopwood, Bell
Experimental Cookery, Brown & Cameron, Edward Arnold
Food Commodities, Davis, Heinemann
Food Hygiene Regulations, HMSO
Food and Nutrition, A Tull, Oxford University Press

Food Preparation, Finch & Cracknell, Pitman
French for Catering Students, John Grisbrooke, Edward Arnold
Kitchen in Catering, Walley, Constable
Human Nutrition, Motram, Edward Arnold
La Technique, Pepin & Brunet, MacMillan
Le Répertoire de la Cuisine, Saulnier, Jaeggi
Manual of Nutrition, HMSO
Modern French Culinary Art, Pellaprat, Virtue
Microwave Cook Book, Norman, Ebury
New Larousse Gastronomique, Montagne, Hamlyn
Planning for Cook Chill, Electricity Council
Practical Cookery, Ceserani & Kinton, Edward Arnold
Practical Professional Catering, Cracknell & Kaufman & Nobis, MacMillan
Practical Professional Cookery, Cracknell & Kaufman, MacMillan
Theory of Catering, Kinton & Ceserani, Edward Arnold
Questions on Theory of Catering, Kinton & Ceserani, Edward Arnold
The Complete Guide to the Art of Modern Cooking, Escoffier, Heinemann
Understanding Cooking, Ceserani, Lindberg and Kotchevar, Edward Arnold

Food service

Can I Help You – the French Menu explained, Schneider & Capisano, Edward Arnold
Clean Catering, HMSO
Menu French, Atkinson, Pergamon
Menu Terminology, Clarke, Licet
The Waiter, Fuller & Currie, Hutchinson

General

A Manual of Hotel Reception, JRS Beavis & S Medlick, Heinemann
Employee Relations, HCTB
Legal Aspects of the Hotel & Catering Industry, Richards & Stewart, Bell & Hyman
People & Communications, Webb
The Prevention of Food Poisoning, Trickett, S Thornes
Training for Health & Safety, HCTB
Supervisors Handbook, Julia Reay, Hutchinson

GLOSSARY OF TERMS

à la Carte Separately priced menu items which are prepared and cooked to order.

accompaniment Items which are usually served with a particular dish to add to and balance the flavour of the whole meal, e.g. fresh mint sauce with roast lamb.

al dente Any food item which is just cooked and which still has a 'bite' to it.

amino acids There are many different proteins, each a complex molecule. The protein molecules link together to form small units called amino acids.

à l'anglaise English style.

à point An item, e.g. a steak, which is medium well-cooked.

ascorbic acid Vitamin C. Found in fruit and vegetables. Supply is best when the fruit and vegetables are eaten fresh and raw.

au beurre With butter.

au gratin Foods which are sprinkled with cheese or breadcrumbs and then browned under a grill (salamander) or in the oven.

au vin blanc With white wine

au vin rouge With red wine.

barquette Boat shaped toasted bread or pastry base.

baste The continuous coating of food with fat, stock, or wine during cooking. Basting keeps the food moist and prevents shrinkage.

bechamel A basic white sauce, made from a seasoned roux base with the addition of milk.

beurre noisette Brown butter.

bien cuit An item, e.g. a steak which is cooked right through.

bin card A record card for an individual commodity held in stock. The bin card is attached to the storage bin and gives details of when the particular goods were received, quantity received, total quantity in stock and issues made. It gives an instant stock level reading.

bind The combination of several food components which are held together by a binding agent, e.g. whisked egg or sauce.

bisque Fish soup.

blanch The process of bringing vegetables or fruit to boiling point and then halting the cooking process by plunging the items into cold water. Used as a part of mis-en-place or preparation of items for freezing. Deep fried items may be partially cooked and cooled and finished on demand. This part in cooking process is known as blanching.

blanquette A white stew.

bouchée A small puff pastry case.

bouillon Unclarified stock.

bouquet garni A collection of herbs, e.g. parsley, thyme and bay leaf which are wrapped in a muslin bag and used to add flavour to savoury dishes.

brine A salt solution used in the preservation of meat.

brochette On a skewer.

brunoise Fine dice-cut of vegetables.

calorie A unit of heat or energy to be known as a kilojoule.

canapé A small hors d'oeuvre item based on bread.

caramel Burnt brown sugar.

cellulose The coarse part of fruit and vegetables which remains undigested and acts as roughage.

checking system A double or triple system used for recording a diner's order. One copy is kept by the food service operative, another goes to the kitchen or production area and the third goes to cash control if this is a separate point.

clarify To make clear by cooking and straining.

chlorophyll The green colouring found in vegetables.

chlostridium A food poisoning bacteria found in soil, vegetables and meat.

coagulate The setting of protein during cooking. This quality is used to hold food items together e.g. foods which are coated or bound with egg.

confiture Jam.

compote A mixture of fresh or dried fruit stewed in syrup.

concasse Coarsely chopped food items.

contamination Contamination involves the spoilage of food or surfaces by harmful bacteria. Cross contamination occurs when spoilage agents are passed from one food to another or one surface to another. The carriers of contamination can be human, animal, work materials, equipment, and premises.

correcting The adjustment of seasoning, consistency and colour, which takes place during the making of a cooked item to make it perfect for service to the customer.

cover The total number of covers refers to the total number of guests at a function. It also refers to a complete individual place setting at table.

croûton Cubes of toasted or fried bread which are served as an accompaniment to soup or used as a garnish.

darne A cutlet of fish.

decant To gently pour off a liquid leaving the sediment behind.

deficiency e.g. vitamin deficiency means lack of, or shortage of vitamins.

demi glace   A mix of equal quantities of espagnole (brown) sauce and brown stock which are cooked together until the quantity is reduced by half and the flavour concentrated.

devilled   Highly spiced and seasoned.

digestion   The process by which food is broken down in the body into a suitable state for absorption and use.

dirt   Dirt is dust, soil or waste material which is held by moisture or grease to a surface.

discount   A discount or reduction in the total amount to be paid may be offered when a bill is paid and settled quickly or when a large quantity of goods are bought at any one time.

dish paper   A plain paper used to cover a serving dish, will carry shallow or deep fried food.

disposables   Items which are designed for a single use. Used where high standards of hygiene are required, e.g. hospital, or where staff and facilities do not allow conventional dish washing or cleaning systems to be used.

du jour   Of the day.

duty rota   Is the master plan of staff hours, shifts and activities. It can be a standard plan used on a permanent basis or rotas can be planned on a changing pattern or weekly basis.

entrée   A meat dish, usually served as a main course.

entremets   A sweet.

enzyme   Enzymes act to stimulate the digestive system and assist in the breakup of food and the release of nutrients.

estouffade   Brown stock.

formulation   Recipe formulation involves planning the ingredients to be used in a dish and deciding which method of production to use to give the desired result in quality, quantity, and appeal.

function   A special event for which individual arrangements are made, e.g. a wedding party, celebration dinner, dance or conference.

frappé   An item which is chilled for service.

garnish   Decoration for a completed food item or dish to give it 'eye appeal' for the diner.

gelatine   A soluble protein used for setting cold food items.

guéridon service   A high class form of food service, where the waiter/waitress prepares food from a trolley which is positioned near the diner. Food will be carved, filleted or flambéed by the highly skilled service staff.

gluten   The protein part of flour which when mixed with water and heated provides a firm structure to food, e.g. holds the shape of a loaf.

haché   Finely chopped or minced food.

hors d'oeuvre   A mixture of cold food items (including a range of salads) which are used as first course dishes to start a meal.

invoice   An invoice is a bill. It lists all the items supplied, their costs and the total amount to be paid.

julienne   Fine strips – a cut of vegetables or garnish.

jus lié   Thickened gravy.

jus rôti Unthickened roast gravy.

licensing hours The laws which govern the sale of all alcoholic beverages.

linen Tablecloths, slipcloths, serviettes, trolley cloths, waiter cloths used in the dining room situation. Although called linen most modern items will be made from cotton or polycotton or disposable materials.

magnetron The device which generates microwaves in a microwave oven.

maître d'hôtel butter Butter mixed with chopped parsley and lemon juice and served as a garnish.

marinade A spiced liquid in which meat is soaked to tenderise and add flavour to it.

metabolism The complex collection of chemical reactions which enable the body to carry out the functions required to support life. Basal metabolism is the amount of energy required to keep the body alive when it is completely at rest and warm.

micro organism Small, living plants or animals, e.g. bacteria, moulds, yeasts.

mineral salts (minerals) Mineral elements which are found particularly in vegetables.

mise-en-place Basic preparations for food production or service which are made in advance of requirement – before items are finished for service.

modified starch Specialised starches which are chemically altered (modified to suit a particular purpose, e.g. freeze/flow starches for sauces to be frozen.)

mono sodium glutamate A food additive used with meat products to improve the flavour.

nutrients These are the components of food – carbohydrate, protein, fat, vitamins, minerals, and water – which combine to maintain health.

panada A thick white sauce used for binding and holding other component food items together, e.g. croquettes.

piquant Sharp, biting flavour.

plat du jour Dish of the day.

pH value A scale which shows the degree of acidity or alkalinity, e.g. in food materials and cleaning agents.

prove The process of setting aside yeast items in a warm place to allow them to rise and expand before baking or frying.

purée Food which has been pulped, sieved or liquidised.

réchauffer To reheat an item which has previously been prepared.

reconstitute To replace the water content of dehydrated foods.

reduce To boil a liquid and by reducing the total quantity to concentrate and improve its flavour, e.g. stock.

refresh To make a food item cold by passing it under cold running water.

reference A comment on the individual's work activity and work record which is sent direct on request to a possible new employer who is conducting selection interviews.

regenerate To make fit for eating foods which have been prepared and then chilled or frozen until required.

requisition A requisition is a form for requesting the issue of goods, e.g. from the food store to the kitchen, or the performance of a service, e.g. a maintenance requisition or request.

roux A thickening made by cooking together an equal quantity of fat and flour. It is used as the basis for sauces, soups and savoury meat dishes.

salmonella A food poisoning bacteria found in meat and poultry and human and animal excreta.

saignant An item, e.g. a steak, which is underdone or rare.

sauté To cook quickly by tossing in hot fat.

service charge Service charge is an addition to the selling price of a meal (the meal price already includes VAT). The service charge carries its own additional VAT. Where a service charge is to be made, the customer must be informed before the meal is ordered.

shred Cut into fine strips by hand or mechanical means.

sommelier A sommelier is responsible for the service of all alcoholic drinks which accompany a meal.

staphylococcus A food poisoning bacteria found in the human throat and nose and on hands, sores and open wounds.

starch A carbohydrate found in cereals.

social skills Customer contact skills which ensure polite, pleasant and efficient service to the customer and careful personal presentation and communication from the staff.

station A set of 4–8 tables under the direction and control of station head waiter/waitress who organise the group of staff who work on those tables.

stock rotation The constant movement of goods according to a controlled pattern, to ensure that older goods are used first, and new goods last. It avoids deterioration and loss of goods.

table d' hôte A menu with fixed courses and limited choice. A single fixed selling price covers the whole cost of the meal.

testimonial A written record of the worker's length of service and duties, which is given to the worker as they leave a job. It can be used as evidence of good work when applying for another post. A confidential reference is usually required as well.

velouté A basic white roux sauce made from a blonde roux and any white stock, e.g. ham or chicken.

ventilation The movement of air in the working situation to give a constant flow of cool fresh air coming in and stale air going out. Natural ventilation achieves this through windows, doors and skylights. Artificial ventilation systems use extractor fans and air conditioning.

vitamins A range of chemical substances which are vital to regulate and control the body processes.

vol au vent A round or oval puff pastry case – larger than a bouchée.

INDEX